Patch Lane

Between the Lines
PUBLISHING

Between the Lines Publishing, LLC

Published by Between the Lines Publishing, LLC (USA) Liminal Books
(imprint)
410 Caribou Trail, Lutsen, Minnesota 55612, USA

www.btwnthelines.com

Cover artist: Suzanne Johnson

Patch Lane
S.F. Barkley

Paperback ISBN: 978-1-950502-15-8

Hardcover ISBN: 978-1-950502-16-5

Also Available in Ebook format

This book is dedicated to all the police officers who keep us safe, especially the two that I love most: my dad and my husband.

Dad,
Thank you for lovingly and patiently guiding me through my life journey. I admire and respect you more than anyone else in this world- you are my inspiration.

Tim,
You are my rock and my best friend. Thank you for supporting me every step of the way. Home is wherever we are together- I love you.

Chapter 1

I pulled into the station's parking lot and glanced down at my watch. 2301 hours. *Shit. I'm late.* I jerked my steering wheel to land in the first open space I saw, threw my car into park, and took one last swig of my room temperature coffee before making a run to the station's rear door. I quietly pulled it open and peeked down the short hallway into the roll call room. The guys were staring at me, apparently anxious to begin roll call.

Before my foot even crossed the door's threshold, Sergeant Oakley announced, "Well, look at that! Hastings decided to show up for work tonight." He paused before adding, "Now that everyone is finally here, may we begin?"

I bit my tongue so hard that I tasted a hint of blood. Why was the focus on me? I was only *one* minute late! Meanwhile, Peterson was sitting right behind me with only half of his duty belt secured to his uniform and his vest wasn't even on yet. That's the thing with cops. We never want to hear complaints or excuses; we just want to know it won't happen again. I offered a half-assed apology. "Sorry, Sarge."

Sergeant Oakley continued with roll call, reading the daylight shift's reports to the five of us who were working the night shift. He briefed us about an ATV accident, a barking dog complaint, and one disorderly conduct citation. Overall, it was a normal, run-of-the-mill roll call.

Amber Forest is a small, predominately agricultural town nestled in the Western Pennsylvania mountains. Our daily reports are rarely exciting. Our chief's mission statement is to "keep the town happy." Sometimes it seems like he adopted this philosophy to avoid paperwork and conflicts with the town council. When they were happy, everyone was happy. Chief wasn't one to disagree with the council or call in the State Police for assistance. He preferred to keep things local.

Sergeant Oakley broke us from roll call, and I walked outside to my cruiser.

"Hey Sarah, you taking the breaching kit?" Peterson asked.

Lazy bastard. He's just asking me, so he doesn't have to carry it from the station to his car. "Yeah, I'll go back inside and grab it. Wouldn't want you to hurt yourself, now would we?"

"I'm too pretty to lift heavy things," he teased.

My shift mates and I have never had a problem calling each other out on things. One of my dad's former female partners gave me a piece of advice that I'll never forget: *"Sarah, if you don't act differently than the guys, then they won't treat you differently."*

I grabbed the breaching kit and hit the road. I grasped the steering wheel and felt something sticky. I've always been more of a tomboy than a "girly girl," but man, some guys could be downright disgusting. At the first red light, I grabbed one of my Lysol wipes from my bag and quickly wiped down the steering wheel. I was sitting in my usual hiding spot to catch some speeding cars on one of the local roads when Dispatch interrupted.

"Dispatch to 1034." Of course, they called the rookie first. I'd been on the department for over a year, but with less than thirty officers in the entire department, I'd unfortunately be labeled the rookie for a while.

"1034, go ahead," I responded with annoyance.

There was a time when I used to jump on the radio eager to respond to calls, but I'd started to burn out. Night after night I dealt with the same drunken idiots and same obnoxious neighbors. I fell in love with the idea of helping people and solving crimes, but I almost never got to do either of those things. The most satisfactory arrests were DUIs, because I knew I could potentially be saving someone else's life by taking that driver off the street. I'd reached the point where I was counting down the days until I had enough experience to try for a detective's spot.

Dispatch was quick to respond. "We got a 911 hang up from a landline that's coming back to 52 Patch Lane. No response on callback."

"10-4. Show me en route."

I started driving down Route 86 toward the address. The call didn't warrant using my lights and siren, but that didn't mean I couldn't have a little fun. I let my foot ease down on the pedal, slowly increasing my speed and heart rate. I guided my cruiser into each bend, attempting to hit every apex. Needless to say, it was a fast six-mile trip. As I neared the location, the Patch Lane street sign came into view, and I made the right turn onto the gravel lane. After about seven seconds of driving in total darkness, the house appeared up ahead on the right with no lights on inside. If it weren't for the moonlight, I wouldn't have been able to see it at all. I parked my cruiser on the side of the road and turned off all of my lights. In training, we were taught to park a safe distance away from a residence. That way, if someone inside decided to ambush us, then we'd have an opportunity to find cover and radio for backup.

I cautiously approached the old farmhouse and felt a wave of chills immediately shoot down my spine. *Who the hell lives here?*

The house was in total disrepair. The exterior had white wooden siding with loosely attached, rotting black shutters. The moonlight highlighted the chipping paint, making the shutters appear two-toned. The old brick chimney was pulling away from the side of the house, and small trees were growing on the lower roof. There were no signs of life inside—no lights, no sound, not even a car parked on the property. It was the only house on the lane, so I deduced this was once a running farm. This must have been the original farmhouse. I slowly made my way around the house, trudging through the overgrown grass, to check the perimeter. With no evidence of life or habitation, I was beginning to question if Dispatch had gotten the address wrong. I got on the radio. "1034 to Dispatch."

"Dispatch, go ahead."

"I'm at 52 Patch Lane. Can you confirm this is the address?"

"Stand by." After about a minute, Dispatch got back on the air. "1034, yes, that's the correct address. Do you need backup?"

"Negative. It appears no one is home, but I'll update."

At this point, I knocked on the front door and announced myself. "Officer Hastings, Amber Forest Police Department!" No answer. All of the windows were closed, so I tried the front door. Locked. I didn't have any extenuating circumstances that would allow a warrantless entry, so all I could do was leave. There wasn't even enough for me to write a police report.

"1034 to Dispatch," I radioed again.

"Dispatch, go ahead."

"It looks like this house is abandoned. I think the 911 hang up might have been some crossed telephone wires. Clear me from the call with no report."

"10-4."

I began driving back down the gravel lane when another wave of chills shot through me. I hit my brakes and glanced in my rearview mirror. My brake lights flooded the house in red, and for a split moment I thought I saw someone standing in the window watching me leave. I blinked, and the figure vanished. My intuition had kept me alive this far, but I knew Chief Fox would rip me a new one if I tried to enter that house based on my intuition and faintly seeing shadows. I took a deep breath and convinced my foot to ease off of the brake and back on the gas.

Is this shift over yet? I looked down at the clock and realized that I still had over half a shift to kill. Just the right time for another cup of coffee. I swear, sometimes caffeine kept me alive as much as my body armor did. I headed over to Pick'n'Go, the local twenty-four-hour gas station, and found two of my coworkers standing there fueling up on caffeine.

"Well, aren't you two busy?" I cracked with an eye roll and a smile.

Peterson and Kingston grinned. "You have fun responding to the ol' doc's house?" Kingston asked.

Clearly, I must have had a dumb look on my face, because Peterson then asked, "You don't know, do ya?"

"Know what?"

"That old farmhouse belonged to Dr. Werner," he responded. "He was the guy who used to do botched abortions and all sorts of inhumane procedures back in the 1800s. You really mean to tell me you haven't heard the stories about him?"

I shrugged. I hate to admit when I don't know something or, even worse, when I'm wrong.

"All the rich used to go to him when they had young daughters getting knocked up or when they had a special needs child they didn't want to keep. He built that house himself. Even named the road Patch Lane as a joke on all the *patching* he did for people. Rumor has it that the old farmhouse is haunted."

"You guys are idiots." I chuckled at the old tale the guys were trying to pull over on me. I wasn't going to let them spook me. Being one of the only females on the department means I have to have skin twice as thick as my male counterparts. I headed over to the coffee pot and poured myself a large steaming cup. No sugar and no creamer— just bold and black, the way I like it.

The rest of my shift was pretty quiet, and by 0700 hours I was more than ready to see my bed. I swung open the front door to my apartment and was greeted with silence. I liked living alone, but sometimes the silence was too loud. I turned on the television in my bedroom for an audible break. I contemplated making a snack, but I didn't want to add dirty dishes to a sink that was already hosting a balancing act. Instead,

Patch Lane

in one swift motion I stripped the thirty-five pounds of gear off my body and crawled into bed.

Chapter 2

I woke up late in the afternoon and refreshed myself with a long, hot shower. I took a deep breath, filling my lungs with steam. *I wish I could stand here all day and skip work.* I closed my eyes, tilted my head back, and gave myself a massage as I shampooed my hair. I remembered reading that finishing with a short burst of cold water helped wake you up, so I gave it a try and instantly regretted my decision. After a shrill scream, I turned the water off and promised myself to never use cold water again.

The dirty dishes in my sink were starting to attract fruit flies. I'd had no motivation to clean my apartment lately, and it showed. I figured now was as good a time as any to tidy up my place. I live on the first floor of a house that was converted into a duplex a few years back, and although it isn't anything special, it feels like home. I have a small deck that overlooks the creek, and I find myself on my deck more than in my family room when it's nice outside. There's something about the sound of running water and the taste of a chilled Riesling that simply complement one another so well.

I instantly felt relief and satisfaction wash over me once my apartment was nice and clean. I had more motivation after I was done cleaning than before. I stood on my deck for a few moments to take in the cool breeze and the sound of the creek. I could've stayed there all day.

I took my phone out of my pocket and saw I had a text from my Aunt Maggie.

Surgery went great. He'll be in room 1211 if you want to stop by before work.

Oh shit! I'd forgotten that my dad had knee surgery that morning. I'd been losing track of time ever since I started working night shift. I checked the time and saw I still had several hours left before my shift began.

I grabbed my uniform and gear and threw them into my car. I headed to the hospital to check on my dad and spend some quality time with him. I made sure to give myself more than enough time to see my dad, change into uniform, and make it to work early. I definitely didn't want to risk being late after the previous day's incident with Sergeant Oakley. I rolled my eyes remembering his reaction to me being one minute late.

"Sarah!" My dad was so excited to see me.

"Hey, Dad, how are you feeling?"

"They have me so drugged up that I don't feel a thing."

He wore a goofy smile and stared at me through glossy eyes. It was weird to see my dad so loopy. "Well, I came by to stay with you until my shift starts. What do you say to a game of checkers?" I reached into my oversized bag and pulled out my old checkers board.

"I'd say that sounds perfect!" My dad grabbed the board out of my hands and started to set it up on the tray table next to his bed. Checkers has always been one of our favorite games. Every time I set up the board, I'm taken back to being seven years old and sitting on the floor next to our old coffee table while my dad sat on the couch. I dragged the corner chair next to my dad's bed, took off my shoes, and tucked both of my legs under my body to assume the position.

I beat him in two rounds before he accepted defeat. He turned on the television, and we sat there watching it, making fun of all of the overly dramatic plots of "reality" shows.

During a commercial break I asked, "When are you supposed to return home?"

My dad thought for a moment. "I think they said within forty-eight hours or so. Since I live alone, they want to keep me here a little bit longer."

I knew he didn't mean for his response to sound accusing, but I already felt guilty for moving out and leaving him alone in our old house. I knew he was lonely, but I also knew that I was an adult and couldn't spend my entire life living with my dad. "Dad, you know I'm happy to come stay with you while you heal."

"Oh, I know. I didn't mean anything by that. I just didn't want you to think I'm staying here for almost a week because there were issues with the surgery. Everything went as smooth as possible. Sweetie, even if you lived with me, you still have a full-time job that takes up most of your day. Well, most of your night. You know what I mean."

I laughed and told him I understood. I pulled out two cheesesteak hoagies from my bag and slyly slipped one onto my dad's tray. "I thought you could use some real food for dinner tonight," I said as I winked and smiled.

My dad's eyes lit up. "With fries on it?" he asked.

"Come on now. Can you eat a hoagie any other way?" I laughed as I started to unwrap one and took a large bite.

"You don't by any chance have some beer in that magical bag of yours, do you?"

"Dad, no. Even if I did, which I don't, no." I shook my head and added, "You can't go mixing beer with meds. You're crazy."

"Oh, I know. Can't blame a guy for trying."

We scarfed down our hoagies and continued to watch terrible television shows. My dad eventually fell asleep around 2200 hours, and I quietly slipped out of the room and started my way toward the station. I made sure to text my Aunt Maggie as soon as I got there and asked her to keep me posted with any updates on my dad. Sweet as always, she assured me she was on her way to spend the night at the hospital with him. Aunt Maggie's text made me feel better, but I still worried about him. Honestly, my dad has always been my best friend, and I wished I had more time to spend with him. He dedicated his entire life to single-handedly taking care of me, and now I could barely find the time to visit him when he had surgery. My gut flipped upside down as I felt the guilt sink deeper.

As soon as I put on my duty belt, I cleared my mind. Cops can't afford distractions when they're at work, especially when those distractions are their own thoughts.

Sergeant Oakley ran us through roll call before dismissing us and telling us to hit the road. We hadn't even left the parking lot before we all heard the tone drop. My right hand shot down to my control panel, ready to activate my lights and siren.

"Dispatch to all units. Please respond priority for a vehicle accident on Route 86 eastbound just prior to mile marker twenty-six."

Before the dispatcher finished her sentence, I had already flipped the switch. My lights were on and my siren was wailing as I sped to the scene of the accident. When I arrived, there was a small silver sedan wrapped around a telephone pole a few yards off the main highway. The ambulance and fire truck both beat me to the scene and were already working to remove the passenger from the vehicle. I threw my cruiser into park, blocked traffic, and ran toward the vehicle.

She was young, most likely still in high school, lifeless behind the wheel. Firefighters were able to remove her from the vehicle, and medics immediately began working on her. Even if the odds of survival are against us, we always try to save lives, because sometimes we get lucky and can bring them back. The medics strapped the CPR machine to her, and I watched as it slammed her chest down and rose back up, like her body was nothing more than a dog toy. They loaded her into the ambulance and drove through the ocean of blue and red lights.

I refocused my attention to the car and began processing the scene with my fellow officers. I noted the location of tread marks, their length, and the direction the vehicle was traveling. One of the other officers followed the driver to the hospital and, sadly, ultimately ended up at the Medical Examiner's office. We try to save lives the best we can, but more times than not, I felt like I was merely cleaning up messes.

Sergeant Oakley walked over and announced that the girl was pronounced dead at the hospital after a couple of hours. Once it became a fatal accident scene, we were forced to call the State Police to take over. Since Sergeant Oakley couldn't keep all of his officers tied up holding the scene until State Police arrived, he cut me loose around 0200 hours. I began patrolling the streets for any DUIs, especially since we had potentially just processed a DUI-related fatality. As I said before, Amber Forest is a pretty quiet town with little to do except drink, so DUIs are one of our biggest problems. I once arrested a guy for driving his tractor drunk down Main Street as he was on his way to buy more alcohol at the local beer distributor. When I stopped him, he had no problem admitting he had been drinking. He explained I could only arrest him for a DUI if he was driving a car or truck, *not* a lawnmower. After a tense discussion and review of the PA DUI code, followed by a jailhouse discussion with Sergeant Oakley, he finally realized that driving or riding anything after drinking was illegal. Who knew that Pennsylvania was one of the few states where even riding a bicycle drunk is illegal? What could I say? This was my hometown, and I wanted to keep it safe from both criminals and idiots.

Around 0230 hours I got another call.

"Dispatch to 1034."

"1034, go ahead."

"We got another 911 hang up from the same number as last night. This time someone stayed on the line, and we could hear someone talking but couldn't make it out. Please check this address out again."

"Can you confirm the address again?"

"It comes back to 52 Patch Lane."

I began to suspect the guys were getting Dispatch to help them with some type of joke, but it didn't matter; I still had to respond. Better safe than sorry. During the drive over, I started plotting ways to get even with the guys for playing this prank on me. The only thing that kept this job entertaining was my relationship with those guys. They weren't just my brothers in blue, they were like my real brothers.

I conducted my normal routine and proceeded to knock on the door and announce myself, "Officer Hastings with the Amber Forest Police Department!" I was about to leave when, out of sheer habit, I checked the door handle. To my surprise, the door opened. I was so startled that my right hand shot down to my gun on my right hip. I prepared for entry and announced myself again. "Officer Hastings, Amber Forest Police Department! Come to the front door!"

No response.

"1034 to Dispatch."

"Dispatch, go ahead."

"No one appears to be home, but the front door was unlocked. I'm going to make entry and check the house. It appears abandoned, though. Do we have any backup available?"

"1034, all units are still on the fatal accident holding the perimeter. Do you need one to break?"

Goddamn, it takes the Staties forever to get on scene. "Negative. I will advise."

I didn't want to ask officers to break from the scene of a fatal car accident to search an abandoned house. I could do it myself. I unholstered my gun and held it at the low-ready position. I cautiously proceeded through the first floor, dodging cobwebs and stepping over dead insects and critters. There was a rickety set of old narrow stairs, and I continued my search upstairs. I checked the bedrooms, closets, and anywhere a person could hide. No one was there. I worked my way back downstairs and proceeded to check the basement. It was fairly small, but it was divided into several tiny rooms. One room had a metal door with a padlock on it. The padlock, which was covered in cobwebs, needed a key to open and was completely corroded and rusted shut. A large, black spider was guarding the lock, apparently having made it its home. This lock had to have been there for years, maybe decades. I bent down and took a closer look at it.

While I was inspecting the lock, floorboards creaked above me. Since there was no way a person was hiding in the locked room, I headed upstairs to investigate the footsteps. I cleared the first floor and worked my way to the second floor again. I finished searching the house not once, but twice. I must have heard a mouse or another critter run around while I was in the basement, because there absolutely wasn't anyone else in that house. I attempted to lock the front door on my way out, but as I went to turn the interior lock, I realized the only way to lock the front door from the outside was with a key.

As I drove away, I got back on the radio. "1034 to Dispatch."

"Dispatch, go ahead."

"The residence was abandoned, and I concluded my search with negative results. I was unable to secure the location because it could only be locked using a key. Can you please attempt to find the keyholder for this location to notify them of the incident?"

"Received."

It's protocol that after we search an unoccupied residence, we have to at least attempt to lock it on our way out. Dispatch usually uses the white pages to try to contact the previous owner, but if they're unsuccessful, then we attempt to run the address through one of our database systems. If we're lucky enough to find a report, then we check to see if there are any associated persons or phone numbers.

Approximately three minutes after I left the scene, Dispatch got back on the radio. "Dispatch to 1034."

"1034, go."

"We were unable to contact a keyholder for 52 Patch Lane. We actually were unable to even find the name of the property owner."

I responded, "Okay, thank you."

I headed back to the station to use one of our computers to run 52 Patch Lane through our database system. I typed in the address and clicked "Submit." To my surprise, the next screen read "No Results." Usually I'd find at least a trespass or graffiti report on abandoned properties, but there wasn't a single police report taken for 52 Patch Lane.

I opted to go grab a cup of hot coffee around 0400 hours and met up with my friend Tim, who had remained on the fatal accident. "Hey Tim, what ended up happening with that DUI crash?"

Tim blew on his coffee to expedite cooling. "We searched through the wreckage and, wouldn't ya know it, we found a water bottle half full of vodka on the floorboard. We notified ME's office and made sure they knew to screen for alcohol levels in our vic." Tim's coffee must have cooled to his liking, as he took a sip. "When the hell will these kids realize the dangers of drinking and driving? Anyway, what did you have over at Patch Lane? I heard you call out that you made entry."

"I'll tell you what, that house is pretty damn creepy. I think these 911 hang ups are crossed wires somewhere in the telephone system." Tim was the only one I would admit being creeped out to, since I know him from when my dad was still on the force. Tim has always treated me less like a coworker and more like a daughter.

"I was just curious because I used to frequently get dispatched for 911 hang up calls to that house, too. It was different back then, though."

I was surprised to hear that Tim had been to Patch Lane before, since I hadn't found any reports in our system. "Oh really? What happened when you went there?" I asked. I've always been naturally curious, and I like to think that helps make me a good cop.

"I bet it's been over twenty years since I was there. I got dispatched there almost once a week, if not more, for about a month straight. There was a young girl living there back then. She had a baby, too. Each time I was dispatched, she would be surprised to see me but also relieved. She always let me search the house without any issues, and she told me

14

she never called 911. I remember she always offered me cookies and coffee afterwards. I never had any problems with her."

"What happened to the woman and her child, then?"

Tim's eyes wandered up and to his left as he tried to remember. "I don't think anything, really. One day they were there, and the next they weren't. I think she might have moved away after ten months or so. A few new families moved in and out renting the house, but ever since the late '90s nobody else has moved in."

I kept thinking about the locked room in the basement and knew it was a stretch, but I asked Tim, "Do you happen to remember there being a locked room in the basement?" I honestly don't know what I was expecting as a response.

Tim's eyebrows raised and he responded, "You know what? I actually didn't remember until you just asked. Yeah, wow. Yeah, the only reason I remember is because the nice girl that lived there with her child didn't have a key and couldn't get into the room. She asked me if I knew a local locksmith, but I told her I didn't really know one since anytime the cops need to get in somewhere, we just smash the lock open. She giggled at my poor attempt at a joke. I remember she was a very attractive-looking girl."

"Tim, did you have a crush on that girl?" I always teased Tim.

"Damnit, Hastings."

We both laughed it off. Though we found the lock odd, we moved on with our shift into the early hours with another DUI stop. Tim pulled a guy over for driving without his headlights, and I backed him up. Tim attempted to instruct the guy how to perform the DUI walk-and-turn test, but he kept getting interrupted.

"You pig. You think you're tough shit with that badge, huh?" the guy slurred as he swayed side to side.

Tim was cool and calm and continued with his instructions.

"I'm not doing any of your stupid tests! I'm leaving!" The guy turned around and started to walk toward the sidewalk.

I had absolutely no patience left. Between the lack of sleep and constant chaos at work, I was in no mood to deal with this guy's bullshit. I swept my left arm under his right arm from behind and held him in a rear armbar.

"Listen here," I whispered. "You're going to do *exactly* what Officer Briggs tells you to do."

The guy screamed in pain.

"You know what? I've changed my mind." I grabbed my handcuffs with my left hand, slapped the cuffs on his wrists, and loaded him into Tim's cruiser.

Tim shut the cruiser door and stared at me. "Jesus, Sarah. You know that guy or something?"

Yeah, I know him. "Nah, he's just one of the usual idiots in this town. He refused to perform the test, so why shit around when we can arrest him? We have enough without the tests."

"Oh, I'm not disagreeing with you at all. I'm just not used to seeing you that aggressive with a suspect." Tim shrugged his shoulders. "I mean, you're good. I'm just surprised is all."

Tim was right. While it was no surprise I stopped the guy from leaving, it wasn't like me to lose my patience. He was just being drunk and stupid; he wasn't a real threat. But what Tim didn't know was that I had stopped that same guy a month ago for drinking and driving. He had given me some sob story about how his sister had just died, so I'd given him a ride home and let him go after he promised he would never do it again.

People are so damn predictable.

Chapter 3

Sergeant Oakley took an extra minute at the end of roll call to emphasize the importance of conducting traffic stops. The crash from the previous night troubled him.

"Listen. We are having kids killed on our roads because of drinking and driving. I know that parents won't be happy if we arrest their perfect little angels for DUIs, but they're gonna be a hell of a lot worse off if their children are killed because they are either drinking and driving, or because someone else under the influence hits them. We need to be proactive instead of reactive. Stop every suspicious vehicle you see for any violation. If you see they have a headlight out, if they rolled through a stop sign, stop them. Ask them all the questions you're taught, like where are they coming from? Where are they going to? Have they had anything to drink tonight? Come on, stay on top of it, team! Alright, now get out there and protect this community."

We all headed outside and racked our cruisers. We focused on pulling traffic with only a few interruptions until Dispatch sent us to some domestic dispute calls and one barking dog complaint. Overall, it was a pretty calm first half of shift. Right until around 0300 hours, when Dispatch called.

"Dispatch to 1034."

I keyed my mic and responded, "1034, go ahead."

"We have another 911 hang up from 52 Patch Lane. Are you able to go?"

I was in the middle of eating my lunch and really didn't want to go. I'm not sure if you could call eating at 0300 hours "lunch," but I wasn't sure what else to call the routine meal. I tried to get out of responding to Patch Lane again and answered, "Yeah Dispatch, I cleared that house last night and I didn't even see a landline. Stand by." I got back on the air and called Sergeant Oakley. "1034 to 1050."

"1050, go ahead."

"Can you switch to channel two?"

I turned my radio to channel two, which wasn't monitored by Dispatch. "Hey Sarge, did you hear this call? Do you need me to go or can we clear it?" I was hoping Sergeant Oakley would give me the okay to not respond, since these 911 hang up calls seemed to be coming from an abandoned house.

"1034, just drive by. No need to go in if you don't see anything, but at least drive by."

"Received. Show me en route." *So annoying.* I didn't even get to finish eating. I switched my radio back to channel one and headed back to Patch Lane for the third night in a row.

This time, the front door was wide open. I was positive that I'd shut it the night before when I left. At this point, I began to think a homeless person was inside, which would be considered trespassing. I contemplated calling for backup, but decided I was going to make entry first, and depending on what I found inside I could always call for backup later.

I called out to Dispatch, "1034, I have an open door. I'm going to make entry."

Dispatch responded, "1034 received. Do you need backup, and do you want us to hold the air?"

"I'll update if I need backup. Affirmative to hold the air."

Gun drawn; I entered the house. Goosebumps trickled down my arms and I looked to my left. Someone ran around the corner and disappeared. All I could make out was a black shadowy figure. "Police! Don't move!"

When I turned the corner, I was in the kitchen. The only way out was a door to the basement.

I got on my radio and requested backup. "1034 to Dispatch. I have someone inside the residence, send an additional unit."

No response.

I continued and carefully made my way around the basement door. I started on one side of the door frame and, working my way in a half circle pattern, crossed to the other side. This "pie" method of clearing a doorway was taught in the police academy to see the maximum area of a room in one swift motion. I couldn't see anyone in the basement. I cautiously walked down the staircase, step by step, with my gun still drawn. No one was there. No one. I got on my radio again. "1034 to Dispatch, I have someone inside the house. Send me backup."

No response.

"1034 to Dispatch, did you copy?" I was yelling into the mic by this point.

No response.

My heart was pounding out of my chest. There was no way out from the basement. I remembered from when I checked the perimeter that the rear door had been boarded up from the outside. Just to be sure, I walked over to the door and tried the handle. The door didn't move.

I made my way back upstairs into the kitchen. I still didn't hear Dispatch respond on the radio. I finished clearing the house and never found the person who ran into the kitchen when I first made entry. I returned to my cruiser and grabbed the radio. I was out of breath at that point.

"1034 to Dispatch."

"Go ahead."

"Did you hear any of my calls for backup?" My agitation traveled through the radio.

"Negative, 1034. You need units?"

"No, you can disregard. I had one subject on the premises, but they're gone. I'm heading back to the station."

When I got back to the station, almost all my fellow officers were anxiously waiting to ask me about what happened. All I could say was that the person I saw inside the house must have run out when they saw me. I didn't tell anyone that the direction the person ran left them absolutely no way of escaping. I began to wonder if I was going crazy. *Did I just see a ghost?* I still had one more shift before my weekend, which consisted of Tuesdays and Wednesdays. Until then, I needed to keep my shit together.

Chapter 4

Finally, my last shift before a couple days of rest. All I could think about was my dad. Aunt Maggie assured me every day that he was in good hands, but I still wanted to be there for him.

"So, you have a hot date at Patch Lane?" Peterson asked.

"You know what? I'm done. One of you assholes can take the next call to Patch Lane." I was annoyed and tired of being sent to the same house every night while nobody else had to deal with it.

"Aww, somebody's cranky." Peterson was merely joking, but I wasn't in the mood. In hindsight, I was probably a bit harsher than I should have been, but they were used to my snappy comments, so nobody seemed fazed by my attitude.

Once roll call broke, I even walked upstairs to Dispatch's unit and told them if they got another 911 hang up from Patch Lane to send it to someone else, because I was getting fed up with those calls. I knew I was the rookie, but that didn't mean I needed to handle every single one of these nuisance hang up calls. Let someone else clear them for once.

Around 0300 hours Dispatch got on the air. "Dispatch to 1045."

Tim responded, "1045, go."

"We got a 911 hang up for 52 Patch Lane. Sarge gave the okay to just drive by and make sure no one is there."

"1045, okay, show me en route."

Not even thirty seconds went by and my cell phone beeped. I had a text.

Hey. Wanna meet me there?

Goddamn it, Tim. I never refuse to back up a fellow officer. I agreed and headed towards Patch Lane.

"1034 to Dispatch, you can add me to 1045's call."

Dispatch acknowledged my request, "10-4."

I could only imagine the comments Dispatch was making upstairs after I'd made a scene telling them not to send me to Patch Lane, and there I was, requesting to be sent there. *Ugh.*

We arrived at the same time and, again, the front door was wide open. As we slowly approached the house, I turned to Tim and quietly instructed him, "Briggs, I already checked the perimeter yesterday and the only way in is through the front door. Let's make entry together." I noticed that the more intense a situation was, the more likely I was to use a coworker's last name rather than first.

Tim agreed, "Alright, Hastings. On me."

Tim announced himself and I followed closely behind as we made entry. We both cleared the first floor, then the top floor, and made our way into the basement together. Nothing. We turned the corner in the basement and found the lock from the metal door was lying on the ground. Someone had cut it with bolt cutters. We looked at each other and Tim asked, "I thought you said this door was still locked?"

"Uh. It was." My eyes widened and I felt my heart race faster.

Tim slowly opened the door, and we were immediately hit in the face with the most horrid smell...a smell I knew well. The smell of death.

We found the corpse of a woman, bloated and fresh.

I knew the body naturally bloated after death and retained trapped gases, which was where the odor originated. That was how I knew it was fresh. Tim called for backup and for Medical Examiners.

The Forensic Investigators from the Medical Examiner's office processed the scene and began to remove the body. One of them turned to me and asked, "Are you Officer Briggs?"

"No, I'm Officer Hastings. Tim Briggs is my partner who was with me on scene." I pointed over towards Tim. "That's him."

"Ah, alright. Is he primary or are you, then?"

I thought for a moment. "He's supposed to be primary, but I think I'm gonna take this one over." It was expected for the rookie to take primary responsibilities for calls that were heavy in paperwork. Plus, I'd been to this house four nights in a row now.

"You got a card?"

I handed the investigator my business card with my contact information. I was curious and asked, "Hey, how long do you think the body has been in there?" After all, they were the experts on this subject matter, not me.

The investigator responded, "Well, this body is in the decomposition phase. She's pretty bloated and rigor has totally diminished. Given this April weather, the temperature has been pretty mild. I would say she's been dead for about three to four days. The official autopsy report will give you a better idea."

It was impossible for anyone to have been in that room in years, hell, in decades because of that lock. I voiced my thoughts, "There's no way that's possible. Well, unless someone moved the body into this room after she was already dead."

The investigator shook his head. "No, there's no way someone dragged that body in here within the past twenty-four hours. You can see the lividity, the pooling of blood on the body, which is consistent with the position she's in right now. You can also see all the fluids on the ground here that her body slowly released. There's already skin slippage occurring, so for someone to drag and move this body in here would be a messy job and she would be in much worse shape."

"But this room was completely locked yesterday. I'm telling you, that isn't possible."

"Listen, it isn't our job to explain why or how the body ended up here, that's your job. All I can say is that this body has been in this room for about three to four days."

Chapter 5

I woke up to an obnoxious ringing coming from my nightstand. I smacked my alarm clock, but it didn't stop the noise. I finally realized, with half an eye open, that it was my phone.

I answered, "Hello?"

"Hastings. Wake the hell up. Chief wants to see you, *now.*"

Ugh. Sergeant Oakley's voice was not what I wanted to hear first thing in the morning, especially on my day off. I glanced at my clock and realized I only slept for about two hours. I rolled out of bed and began to get ready to head into the station, since I knew it was never a good sign when good old Chief Fox wanted you in his office ASAP.

Around 1030 hours I walked into the station and began making my way to the stairwell to head upstairs to Chief Fox's office. My handcuffs jingled rhythmically with every step. I knocked on the chief's open door and poked my head around the corner. Chief Fox fiercely called out to me, "Hastings, come in and shut the door."

I shut the door behind me and took a seat.

"Well, Hastings, you shouldn't be surprised why you're here. You got dispatched to the same goddamn house four nights in a row and discovered a dead body on the fourth night. Then, we find out that this body had been there for several of the previous nights! You really screwed the pooch, Hastings. Now I have paperwork out the ass and you need to answer some questions."

What the hell? How is he turning this thing on me? I did my job, I followed protocol, I followed my training, and I cleared the house as I was taught. "Okay, Chief, what questions do you have?"

"Walk me through the first night. Did you check the windows? The doors?"

"Yes, I checked the windows, which were all secured, and the front door was locked. The only other door was a door to the basement, which was boarded shut. It's a very old and small farmhouse."

"Alright. What about the second night? Windows? Door?"

"Chief, I checked the windows and, as my report says, the second night the front door was unlocked. I followed protocol and made entry."

"And tell me about why you didn't check the room in the basement."

"Well, according to Maryland vs. Buie, I conducted a person sweep of the home to check for any persons on the premises, since the property appeared abandoned. I looked in all areas that a person could potentially hide. When I got to the room in the basement, the lock was rusted, corroded, and covered in cobwebs. There was no way anyone could have hidden in that room and locked themselves inside. I was not searching for a crime or illegal substances since I was only legally allowed to search for persons in that residence."

"I know the goddamn law, Hastings, thanks. Did you try the lock?"

Despite his response, I wasn't convinced Chief Fox actually knew the law as well as he should. I kept my lips shut and took a deep breath through my nostrils. *Don't get fired for losing your cool, Sarah.* Call me crazy, but I don't respond well when people treat me like an idiot. "Well, no. I could see that it would not have opened."

"Did you think to call one of the male officers to try to open the lock?"

Was he serious? Was he actually testing my limits right now? "Chief, the reason I didn't try to open the lock wasn't because I thought

I was too weak. I didn't try to open it because I could tell it had not been touched in decades."

"Well thanks to your self-proclaimed locksmith expertise, this entire case is under scrutiny. I'm gonna be keeping a close eye on you."

"Chief, I followed all of our departmental procedures and stayed within the law. If you feel I handled these calls improperly, then please provide me the additional training and procedures that would guide me on how I should have handled it."

"Nobody likes a smartass, Hastings. Go start your shift. You have a lot of follow ups to do now for this case and can't be doing that shit at night."

What an asshole. I knew from the day the town council hired me that Chief Fox hated me. As I said, it's a small town, so the chief tends to do what the town council tells him to do. Lucky for me, the town council was eager to hire another female officer, but I didn't think Chief was on board with their idea. I was used to the sexism in this small town, but I tolerated it since my fellow patrol officers, for the most part, didn't share the chief's criticism.

I figured since I was already in uniform and at the station, I might as well follow up with the Medical Examiner's office. I wanted to see what information they had from the autopsy and crime scene since we didn't seem to have a copy of their report at our station. They were usually pretty good about getting autopsies done first thing the following morning, and since it was already afternoon, I figured there was a good chance they'd finished it by now. I grabbed one of the phones at the station and called the Chief Medical Examiner.

"Hey, it's Officer Hastings from the Patch Lane case. Did you guys by any chance get to finish up the preliminary autopsy report?"

"Yeah."

"Oh okay, I didn't see a copy here at the station. Can you send it over?"

"I'm pretty busy right now, and plus, that's my assistant's job."

"Alright, how about I swing by and pick it up?"

"You can do whatever your little heart desires."

The Chief Medical Examiner wasn't exactly eager to help, but I grabbed my cruiser's keys and headed on over to the lab. The assistant was a young girl who looked fresh out of college and greeted me with a smile. "Hello, Officer! How can I help you?"

I asked her for a copy of the Medical Examiner's preliminary report from Patch Lane and she proceeded to enter some letters into her computer and hit "Print." She grabbed the papers and handed me a three-page document.

"Aren't there more pages?" I asked.

"Nope. That's it."

I found this very odd considering most medical autopsy reports for a homicide case were well over twenty or thirty pages. Even though I was only asking for the preliminary report, I would still expect there to be several more pages. The official autopsy report took approximately one month, because the lab tests took a while to receive the results. However, the initial autopsy findings and physical evidence were predominately documented in the preliminary report.

I took a seat to look over the report, and I guess I did a poor job of hiding my confusion and anger since the receptionist asked if there was a problem. I was never good at hiding my emotions. As I reviewed the preliminary report, I noticed the hair color, which I remembered clearly as long and blonde, had been listed as "brown," and the eye color was listed as "undetermined." I wished this was the end of the shit show, but the entire report seemed to be either wrong or incomplete. The manner of death was listed as "homicide," but the cause of death was stated as "undetermined." *What the hell?* Wasn't that their job to determine the cause of death?

I marched over to the Chief Medical Examiner's office and knocked twice before walking in. "Chief, is this just a skeleton report from the Patch Lane incident?" I held up the three-page document in my hand to show him. A skeleton report is a basic report cops will fill out prior to end of shift, then the next day they fill in the gaps with fresh eyes. However, with this being a homicide case and now over forty-eight hours old, I didn't understand why they would only have a skeleton report.

"Nope. That's the finished preliminary report, sweetheart." I hate when old creepy men called me sweetheart, but I hate it even more when they don't do their job.

"Well, why is there no cause of death listed?"

"Because, thanks to you, the body sat in a locked room for days and left us barely any evidence to work with."

Why the hell is everyone blaming ME for this!? "Then can you explain why the hair color is wrong and about half of these items are listed as 'undetermined?'" I was not going to back down.

"If you think you can do better, go right ahead."

I stared in silence as I contemplated what I wanted to say next. Well, what I *wanted* to say was that he was acting completely incompetent, but I highly suspected that would get me nowhere in my search for answers. Instead, I played the part of a "sweetheart" and asked to go see the body, because I wanted to make sure I wasn't confusing the details in my head. Shockingly, he agreed and took me over to the cooler. He opened the stainless-steel door and motioned for me to enter. Once I was inside, he quickly exclaimed, "I have a million other things to do. You can see yourself out when you're finished."

It was odd that he left me in the cooler alone with the bodies, but whatever, I went with it. Again, it's a small town, so the morgue only had three bodies in the cooler. I found our Jane Doe from Patch Lane and unzipped the bag, revealing blonde hair...I knew I wasn't crazy. I also noticed that she still had on all her clothes. No autopsy was ever done on this body.

I grabbed a pair of latex gloves and began to go through her pockets to look for identification, since clearly the Medical Examiner's office had decided it was "undetermined" if she had items in her pockets. I found a receipt from a gas station for ten gallons of gas priced at $1.12 per gallon. I started to feel jealous of this dead woman as I wondered where she'd found gas that cheap. Then, I looked to the top of the receipt and saw the date stamp of "10/20/1998." *Why the hell would she keep a receipt that old?* I flipped the receipt over and saw there was some type of writing in pencil on the back, but I couldn't make it out due to all the moisture it was exposed to during the body's decomposition stages. I put the receipt in a baggie and decided I was going to send it out to the Pennsylvania State Police Forensic Lab for further testing, to see if they could decipher what was written. The longer I looked at our Jane Doe, I also noticed that she was wearing bleached jeans with a multicolored sweatshirt, as if she had come straight from the 1990s. Everything about this body felt off.

I picked up her right hand to get a closer look to determine if there were any signs of a struggle. I was startled by the feeling of touching cold flesh. Even though I knew she was dead, there was a natural expectation that the skin would be warm when touched. It wasn't.

I carefully turned her hand to the right, then to the left, looking for any cuts or bruising, but being that I'm not a pathologist, I didn't have the proper equipment or training to test for evidence under her fingernails. I worked my way up the body and stopped at her neck. There was discoloration around her neck. I couldn't make out if it could be from someone's hands or an object, such as a rope. If the Medical Examiner would have just done his damn job then this wouldn't have been an issue. I took as many photographs as I could and scribbled notes in my notepad. It was so cold in the cooler that my pen's ink froze and wouldn't write any more.

I left the cooler when I could barely feel my own fingers. I walked back down the hallway to the Chief Medical Examiner's office.

"Do you have any copies of your attempts to identify the body, like dental moldings, fingerprints, DNA tests, et cetera?"

He handed me a stack of some papers and simply replied, "Good luck."

I flipped through the papers and realized the fingerprint card was only half filled out. "Why are there only six fingerprints? Why didn't you do all ten like normal?" I asked him accusingly.

"Well, why didn't you check the lock on the door while you were at the house three days ago? I don't tell you how to do your job, so why the hell are you gonna try to tell me how to do mine?" He grew louder and angrier.

I wanted nothing more than to scream at him, but I knew my place. Instead, I decided I'd redo her fingerprints myself, since the ones he'd handed me looked half-assed and weren't even complete. My dad always joked that my first sentence was *I can do it myself.*

The Medical Examiner was usually more thorough than this. I had no idea why it was starting to feel like I was the only one even trying to solve this case anymore. I headed back down to the cooler and unzipped Jane Doe's bag again. I carefully fingerprinted all ten of her fingers and ran them through my mobile Automated Fingerprint Identification System, or AFIS. My heart skipped a beat when I saw that I got a hit. Finally, the screen loaded and read:

Michelle Kline
Date of Birth: 07/05/1972
Date of Death: 10/20/1998

That isn't possible. How could that body have been dead for twenty years? It was fresh; I could still smell it. It made absolutely no sense. I hurriedly zipped up the body bag again before I walked out of the cooler and made my way back to my cruiser.

I walked into the station and was greeted by our chief's assistant. "Hello, Officer Hastings!"

Betty Ann was a sweet old woman, but her level of energy was annoying when I was running off two hours of sleep. "Hi, Betty Ann."

Patch Lane

"Oh my, you look awfully tired. You heading home now? How was the Medical Examiner's office?"

I was too drained to even use words, so I nodded my head and waved my hand as I walked past her desk and out to my car.

Chapter 6

I woke up Wednesday feeling groggy with a pounding headache. I was beginning to think the bottle of wine I'd finished the night before wasn't such a great idea. That's the thing with cops—when we come across horrific scenes that we can't rationalize or explain (whether it be murdered children, abusive husbands, finding a twenty-year-dead body…) we turn to alcohol. Me personally, I turned to a nice dark merlot. I couldn't stop wondering how that body could have died twenty years ago. It made no sense.

That day was supposed to be my day off from work, but I couldn't shake my curiosity. I decided to do some digging on Ms. Michelle Kline. I threw on a pot of coffee and flipped open my laptop. I searched every police database system that I had access to. Nothing. I broadened my search to all public websites and could not find one single social media page for Michelle Kline. I searched for white pages, court records, anything that could relate to Michelle Kline. None of my results matched her date of birth or even remotely resembled our Jane Doe. It was as if she was a ghost.

After about three hours, I concluded my search and gave up. It was funny how I spent my entire week looking forward to a day off work, and then I spent half the day working. I couldn't get this case off my mind.

I spent the rest of my night trying to relax. I got out my drawing pad and told myself to draw the first thing that came to my mind. I hadn't drawn anything in months, but I missed it. I missed creating something new and using my imagination. I sat on my couch for hours, drawing and, of course, drinking wine. Lots and lots of wine. Before I realized what I was drawing, I looked down and found a poorly drawn picture of the Patch Lane farmhouse. *Why did I just draw that?* Clearly, I did a poor job at trying to not think about work. I ripped off the page and threw it in the trash.

I wished I was a better artist like my mom was. I kept an old journal of hers that she sketched ordinary things in, but somehow her drawings made these average things look beautiful and unique. My favorite ones were her renditions of a fork, a black cat, and a swing. And here I was, and I couldn't even make an old haunted farmhouse look interesting. I gave up on my efforts and called it a night.

I woke up Thursday ready to head back into work. I grabbed my keys with my left hand while I wedged my right-hand fingers between my duty belt and uniform belt to get my last belt keeper snapped into place before running out the door to make it to roll call on time. While driving to the station, all I could think about was how the only logical solution was that my mobile AFIS was wrong. I decided that, as soon as roll call ended, I was going to grab a different one from the station and scan my Jane Doe's fingerprints again.

Sergeant Oakley ran roll call as normal. He filled us in on the calls that the daylight shift had responded to earlier and announced a couple nationwide officer safety bulletins issued by the FBI. "Tonight," he added, "there's one more thing we need to talk about, too. The body at Patch Lane is still under investigation. I want everyone to make it a point to drive by Patch Lane, since it's still an active crime scene, and make sure no teenagers are trying anything."

I was only half listening to Sergeant Oakley, since all I could think about was running Jane Doe's fingerprints again. As soon as roll call was over, I grabbed one of the newer mobile AFIS devices and racked my cruiser before heading to the Medical Examiner's office.

There was no young, cheery receptionist, since it was the middle of the night. Instead, I had to use a phone hanging on the wall of the entrance to call the forensic investigators who were on duty. A man answered the other end of the phone and told me he would be right out. Nearly two minutes went by before a man with grey hair and stubble walked towards the door and opened it for me.

"What can I do for you, Officer?" the investigator asked.

"I'm working the Jane Doe case from Patch Lane. I was really hoping you could let me take some additional photographs of the body for my investigation." I thought photographs would sound a lot better than asking to run her fingerprints again because last time I tried, a dead woman's name came up.

"Uh, sure. I think she's still in the cooler. She's set to be cremated real soon, though."

Oh God, please let her body still be there. I followed the investigator back to the cooler and he entered behind me. *Shit, how am I going to fingerprint her with him standing right here?*

I reached into my right cargo pocket. "I am such an idiot. I left my camera at the station. Do you have a camera I could borrow?" I was impressed with my lying, because I'd never been good at it before. Again, I used the preconceived notion of being a ditsy woman to my advantage.

"Oh yeah, don't worry about it, I can go get you one. I'll be right back."

As soon as the investigator had left the cooler, I hurriedly took out my AFIS and started scanning her fingerprints again. The machine was running slowly, but it seemed to be thinking. The screen read:

Processing...
Processing...
Processing...

Then, after what felt like eternity (but, in reality, was maybe a minute) the screen read:

35

System has timed out. Failed attempt.

That was weird. This had *never* happened to me before. I decided to try it again. I was rushing so fast that I almost dropped the AFIS as I made my second attempt. This time I could actually feel my heart start to thud louder and louder as I waited for the results.

Processing...

Processing...

No Results Found.

Are you kidding me? I was used to seeing this screen when I scanned a suspect's fingerprints who had never been arrested before and was not in the system. I'm not sure why I was so surprised this time, considering I didn't really believe that Michelle Kline was the correct match in the first place. I still couldn't understand why my AFIS told me the day prior that my Jane Doe was really Michelle Kline, who'd died twenty years ago, then the next day it was telling me that the same prints were not a match to anyone in the database. I also couldn't ignore the fact that Michelle Kline's date of death matched the date of the receipt in my Jane Doe's pocket.

The cooler door opened, and I quickly shoved my AFIS back into my cargo pocket. I thanked the investigator for getting me the camera, took a few random photographs of Jane Doe, and left the Medical Examiner's office.

I didn't tell anyone about my previous Michelle Kline results, because I was convinced that I did something wrong or that the mobile AFIS malfunctioned. Either way, I worried something exactly like this would happen, and I wouldn't have proof of my results and then I would look like an idiot. Since I wasn't getting many questions answered by investigating the body, I decided to return to Patch Lane to try to get some answers from the scene of the crime.

After everything that had happened, I realized it would be smart for me to have backup. I asked Tim if he would be willing to head back over to Patch Lane with me—under the radar. He agreed, and we both advised Dispatch that we would be away from our cruisers and conducting foot patrol around the park. Dispatch was less likely to send a call to us if they knew we weren't near our cruisers. I turned onto Patch Lane and rolled my cruiser to a stop before shutting off the engine. Tim followed suit right behind me. He slowly forced himself out of his cruiser, muttering about his bad back.

"Hastings, what are we even looking for back here?"

"Anything, Briggs. I don't think the ME's office processed the scene properly based on how they handled the body."

"What are you talking about?"

Shit. I hadn't told him about my little visit to the Medical Examiner's office. "Nothing. Let's start out and do a full sweep of the perimeter."

I didn't have one particular thing I was looking for, so I kept my eyes open for anything suspicious. It was pitch black outside, and I could barely see anything except with help from my flashlight. There was still police tape across the front door, with a red sticker on the seal of the doorway stamped "Do Not Enter." I leaned in to check the handle to see if it was locked. As I reached down, I heard a loud, shrill scream directly behind me. I jumped back, spun around, and shined my flashlight straight ahead. Nobody was there. I heard a much softer, quieter squeal come from ground level. I redirected my light downward and sitting in front of me was a cat as black as night.

"Jesus Christ, cat. What the hell are you screaming at me for?"

Memories of my mom referring to black cats as Halloween cats passed through my mind and a faint smile crossed my face. Now that she had my attention, she came up to me and wrapped her body around my leg, purring. I proceeded to check the rest of the windows and worked my way to the rear of the house, towards Tim. The cat followed and began frantically meowing at me the closer I got to the rear of the house. Her screaming got so bad I had to throw her some crackers from my pocket just to distract her. As they say, a good cop is never tired, cold, or hungry. That's why I always had coffee on hand, gloves in my cruiser, and crackers in my pocket.

I stared up at the farmhouse, distracted by imagining the potential beauty that this two-story home could have possessed. My daydreams came to a halt when I noticed a shadow in the upper level window. I squinted, but I couldn't make out what it was. I began stepping backwards to get a better look through the upper level window, all while shining my flashlight towards the window. By about my seventh or eighth step back, I felt something hard and sharp whack the back of my ankle, and it brought me to my knees.

Tim came running over, since this time I was the one doing the yelling and not the cat. He shined his light down to make sure I was okay. Thank God there was no blood and I seemed to be fine. I bent over and repositioned my flashlight to see what I had felt go into my ankle. I saw something protruding from the grass, and when I reached down to pick it up and examine it, I grasped a rusted, sharp chunk of metal. It was an old root cellar door handle. I remembered my grandma telling me about how everyone would use root cellars on these old farms as she laughed at my dad for having a chested freezer in our basement.

"What the hell is that?" Tim asked.

"It's a root cellar door," I told him. "We need to see what's down there."

"Like hell we do."

I shined my light in Tim's eyes and said, "Yes. We do." As much as I love Tim, he can be a bit of a pushover, which I suppose I took advantage of at times. We opened the door and I used my baton to clear the path of spiderwebs.

Tim took a step backwards and said, "Hastings, you're going first."

"And they say chivalry's dead," I mocked as I took a step forward. I put on a brave face, but I was terrified. I magically became braver when I needed to prove a point.

I shined my light down and proceeded one step at a time. I went slowly so as not to fall through one of the old, wooden stairs. We walked down what could only be described as a dirt tunnel for about ten seconds before we reached another small set of stairs. There were about four steps going up that led to a small hatch, almost like an attic door. I reached up and cracked opened the hatch. I popped my head up and shined my light around. There was a large rug over the hatch opening, which Tim helped me push out of the way. Once we could finally see in the room, I was able to recognize it. We'd found Jane Doe in this room.

Tim grabbed my arm. "Hey, Sarah, we really need to go." I knew he was nervous because he rarely used my first name. "This is still an active crime scene. We can't just go walking around inside."

We'd finally figured out how the body got in that room. I knew I wasn't crazy. There was no way anyone had touched the lock on the outside; the corrosion, rust, and cobwebs were absolutely real. We turned around and retraced our steps, careful not to disturb anything. I tried to look for evidence along the way, but it was too dark. I made a mental note that it was an area that would be better examined during daylight.

We returned to our cruisers and calmed our nerves over a long smoke break, despite the fact that I wasn't even a smoker.

Tim and I rode out the rest of our shift at Pick'n'Go, where I went through three cups of coffee while Tim smoked nearly an entire pack of cigarettes. We worked up the courage to tell Sergeant Oakley what we'd found and admitted to lying about calling out on foot patrol at the park.

Sergeant Oakley scolded us, reminding us that the reason it's important to be honest about our location is that in the event something was to happen, our fellow officers needed to know how to get to us. He told us to write a supplemental report to the Patch Lane case with what we'd found and said he would send some guys out in the daylight to further investigate.

Patch Lane

I eventually made my way home and, despite all the caffeine I drank, immediately passed out.

Chapter 7

One thing I loved about working night shift was that there was no brass at the station when I got to work. However, that night was different. As soon as I walked into the station, I overheard the guys talking about some suits that were up in the chief's office. Sergeant Oakley saw me and snapped his fingers at me. "Hastings. Get over here. Chief got called in tonight because of a surprise visit from some suits. He wants you in his office immediately."

Why are there suits here? Local cops refer to federal agents as "suits" because they're a special breed of law enforcement officers who wear suits rather than uniforms.

I headed upstairs to the chief's office, a little surprised that the feds were getting involved in this case. Not to mention, I was shocked they would make a visit in the middle of the night. I began to wonder if the FBI had gotten involved because of a potential serial killer or something more serious. My thoughts were quickly interrupted by Chief Fox. "Hastings! Get your ass in here."

Oh, the wonderful sound of his voice. "Hello, Chief. How can I help?"

"Hastings, the Marshals got called in to help with this case."

...The U.S. Marshals? But they usually go after fugitives. Do they think a fugitive did this to our Jane Doe? Do they think our Jane Doe was a fugitive? My mind was going a hundred miles per minute.

Chief Fox motioned with his hand for me to take a seat in his office. "Hastings, I'm gonna need you to answer any and all questions that these two Deputy Marshals have for you." Chief turned towards the suits. "I'll be down the hallway if you gentlemen need anything further from me." He walked out of the room and one of the suits shut the door.

I couldn't help but notice one of the Deputy Marshals was much more attractive than the other. He couldn't have been much older than I was. He looked like he played a sport, soccer perhaps. He was impeccably dressed and had polished shoes. The second Deputy Marshal was wearing the expected suit and tie, but he clearly didn't share the same tailor as the first. He was shorter and had a belly that was pushing the bottom button of his shirt to its limit. Clearly, he was in denial about his true shirt size.

The short one reached out his hand. "Deputy Jackson. Nice to meet you, Officer Hastings."

I met his handshake with a firm grip and introduced myself. "Thank you. Please feel free to call me Sarah."

The younger U.S. Marshal extended his hand next. "Matthew Sloan." He was much less formal than his partner.

I sat down and walked them through my past week, trying hard to remember every detail. I explained the 911 hang ups and how Tim and I had found the body. I admitted to being perplexed at how the body could have possibly been in that room the previous days until Tim and I found the secret hatch. I had no intention to give them any details about the fingerprints and Michelle Kline, out of fear of sounding crazy or like a rogue cop. They asked me several questions, most of which were answered in my report. I was proud of myself for successfully refraining from telling them that if they'd read my report, they would know half of these answers.

Then, Jackson asked me something that caught my interest, so much that I leaned over the table intently to hear what he was going to say next. He asked, "Officer Hastings, are you familiar with the U.S. Marshals Witness Protection Program?"

I was on the edge of my seat wondering if they were about to put me into Witness Protection. I was thinking through every scenario of what I could have unraveled that would put me in such a dangerous position. Was it the tunnel that I'd found? Was it because of who Jane Doe really was?

I answered their question and explained to the deputies that I understood their Witness Protection Program to be a program for victims and witnesses of crimes who feared for their lives to go into hiding and receive a new identity from the U.S. Marshals.

Jackson and Sloan both nodded their heads. Sloan spoke next. "You basically have the right idea. Well, your Jane Doe was in our WITSEC."

I was speechless. It seemed like every time a question was answered, it created ten more. My Jane Doe was in the Witness Protection Program. Why? Why would she risk her life by leaving WITSEC? Who wanted her killed?

The deputies were extremely professional and appeared as though they wanted to help. They weren't willing to divulge any specifics or details as to why Jane Doe was put into the program or why she may have been killed. They did, however, tell me that she was a key witness to a very high-profile case years ago involving the ATF, the Federal Bureau of Alcohol, Tobacco, Firearms, and Explosives (they would tell you that the "E" was silent). *Maybe she witnessed a bombing. Or maybe she knew someone manufacturing guns.* I couldn't stop as the theories flooded my head.

They also told me that my Jane Doe's real name was Michelle Kline. Deputy Sloan further explained that they faked her death upon entry into the Witness Protection Program so that the suspect she was going to testify against would not go looking for her. He added, "We found out about her real death when we got an alert that someone ran her fingerprints through AFIS. As soon as we got the alert, we tried to cover her identity, since we had no idea she was dead at that point. As soon as we discovered it was someone at this department that ran her prints, we rushed over. We're going to be handling this case with the ATF and FBI on a special joint task force. I am sure we will need your assistance, but we wanted to let you know that we're taking it over from here."

Before I could ask any questions, they shook my hand and thanked me for my time. They walked out the door before I could even get a "why" off my tongue. Who killed Michelle Kline? Who kept calling 911? What did this poor woman get herself into? Why was there a receipt in her pocket from 20 years ago? My questions remained trapped inside my head.

For the rest of my shift, I completed paperwork, which I eventually faxed over to Jackson and Sloan. I got home early Saturday morning and only had two glasses of wine before rolling into bed at 0730 hours. Don't be mistaken, it wasn't that I didn't want to drink an entire bottle again, but I was just too tired.

Chapter 8

Sergeant Oakley treated us to a box of donuts at roll call before we hit the street. I know that cops eating donuts is the biggest stereotype of them all, but who doesn't love donuts?

Before I could finish racking my cruiser, I got the call, "Dispatch to 1034."

"1034, go ahead."

"1034, we got a call from a senior citizen who is currently at her neighbor's house. She is a Medical Alert customer and oxygen dependent. Her phone lines are currently not working, and she is requesting to speak with an officer." Dispatch went on to provide me her address and her neighbor's contact information.

"1034, show me en route."

Although there isn't much for an officer to do on a call such as this, I still had to respond. I drove down the long country road towards the caller. I arrived on scene and saw an elderly woman with an oxygen tube strapped around her ears hanging on to her walker. She opened her screen door and called out to me, "Hello, Officer! I'm Judy, I called you."

This woman instantly reminded me of my own grandmother. "Hi ma'am, I'm Officer Hastings. What seems to be going on here today?" I gave her a big smile and followed her inside her house.

"I already walked to my neighbor's house and called the phone company about my phones not working, but I wanted an officer to keep me company until the they're fixed since I am oxygen dependent. I've already had more than one fall, and I'll tell you what. My Medical Alert saved my life."

"Well, Judy, I'm happy to wait here with you."

She lived in an older farmhouse (there are many of those in this area) and had one of the prettiest farmlands I had seen in a while. Her garden was filled with colorful flowers and cute lawn ornaments throughout. It reminded me of my Aunt Maggie's farm where I spent almost half my childhood due to my dad working so many odd hours. She caught me staring at her flowers and said, "Oh yes, my daughter comes by every week to help keep my garden looking so pretty. Her husband mows the lawn for me, and she tends to my flowers."

I was shocked to see the local phone company drive down the gravel road within thirty minutes of my arrival. I went outside to greet the technician and explained the problem. He introduced himself as Scooter and asked me where the box was located. As quick as I could repeat the question in my head, Judy yelled from the porch, "It's behind the house, near the shed!"

I followed Scooter behind the house and saw the grey box attached to the rear wall. Scooter walked over to it and began reaching to his belt for some tools.

"What is that?" I asked, pointing to the box.

"This is the network interface device. This box connects her telephone line to the central telephone system. I'm going to see if there's a problem with the wires making the connections." He attempted to open the hinge. No luck. "These things usually go months, maybe years, without being opened and take a little TLC to open...*Ah*, there we go."

The front face gave way after a little elbow grease was put into it. The box was filled with several wires of different colors. "So, can you explain to me what's going on here?" I asked out of curiosity.

"Well, these boxes were put here way before your time. They had to install these when landlines were actually used. You see these here?

They connect her landline telephone to the telephone poles, which connect it to the central system."

I noticed a telephone jack in the top right corner of the box. I asked, "And what is the purpose of having a phone jack in this box? Who would have a phone outside?"

"Oh, that's there so the customer can plug their phone in to test the lines. I also have a special phone I can use to test the lines from any of these boxes."

"Wait, what?! You can carry a phone in your pocket, plug it in, and make a call from a box? Does everyone have one of these boxes?"

Scooter laughed and explained, "Yeah, I guess you could put it that way. Everyone who has a landline telephone with wires above ground has one of these. Newer homes with the wires underground have something different. These boxes here are usually used by the customer, though, to check for a dial tone. That lets them know if there's an issue with the lines, or if there's an issue with their phone."

The wheels in my head began to turn. "What phone number would show up if you called someone from this box?"

"Whatever the phone number is of this house's landline," he pointed to Judy's house.

It was then that I had my light bulb moment. What if my 911 hang ups at Patch Lane were being done from one of these boxes? I asked, "So, if a house had no electricity and no telephone, could it still show up as the origin of the phone call if someone made a phone call from a box? Specifically, what if they tried to call 911 from a box?"

Scooter paused for a moment to digest my question. He finally responded, "Uhh...I guess. Yeah, I mean, that's possible. As long as the telephone number has not been reassigned to another person, it would still work."

Scooter finished up his work and was able to get the phones working again. I walked back up to Judy's house and gave her the good news. She was incredibly relieved to hear that her telephones were working again, and she thanked me for my time and patience.

I made the mental plan to go back to Patch Lane in the daylight to see if I could find one of these network interface devices on the farmhouse.

Chapter 9

I called Sergeant Oakley and asked him if I could adjust my hours so that I could visit Patch Lane in the daylight for a follow up investigation. Sergeant Oakley was always supportive when any of us needed to move up our hours to help with a case.

I drove to Patch Lane and sat in my cruiser for a moment. The farmhouse looked so much sadder in the daylight. What once stood as an overshadowing and haunting architecture now sat in front of me as a house ready to fall over. I walked towards the decaying structure to look for a network interface device like the one I saw at Judy's. I checked the front of the house, walked around the left side, and around the back. It wasn't until I'd made almost a complete circle that I found the box on the right side of the house.

I leaned over, wrapped two of my fingers inside the front panel, and pulled. The door opened with ease, unlike the last box I watched Scooter open. Somebody had opened this one recently. But who?

On the way back towards my cruiser, I heard screaming. Goddamn cat nearly gave me a heart attack. I turned around and saw the Halloween cat sitting by the front porch. As I looked at her in the daylight, she looked familiar. Not in the sense that I remembered her from my last visit, but like I'd seen her several times before I visited Patch Lane. This time, she looked in pain. She was holding a front paw in the air and kept licking at it, screaming in pain. I got closer and saw that her paw looked incredibly swollen. Being an animal lover, I decided to wrap her in an old uniform shirt I had in my trunk and set her in my cruiser. I grabbed my phone from my front vest pocket and searched for local veterinarians. I was surprised to see my family's old vet was still open and in business. We had a black lab growing up that I swear was the most intelligent dog. We used to take her to Dr. Demeyers, who could seemingly communicate with pets and know just what was wrong.

Dr. Demeyers was just down the road. I headed towards his office and was grateful when he took us right in and began examining her paw. I couldn't believe this guy was still alive, let alone still working! I remembered him being old when I was a kid. He had to be in his eighties by now. I remembered my dad used to call Dr. Demeyers "The Mayor" because he knew everyone in this town and everything about them. For as much as my dog hated the vet, I swear my dad loved coming here to shoot the shit with Dr. Demeyers.

"And who do we have here, Officer?" I could tell that he didn't recognize me, but I couldn't blame him. It was probably close to ten years since the last time I had been here.

As I stared at the Halloween cat, I said the first name that rolled off my tongue. "Hallie. I found her down on Patch Lane at an abandoned farmhouse. She was sitting on the front porch, crying in pain. I couldn't leave her there."

"Ah yes, I haven't heard about Patch Lane in quite a while."

"Oh, are you familiar with that house?" I asked.

"I don't know if I would say that. I just remember the stories that circulated the town way back when." He stopped to write down some notes in the chart. He looked up and continued his thought. "That was a beautiful place. I remember taking care of the cows on the old Werner Farm when the Goodes lived there."

I remembered hearing about the Goodes passing in the 1980s, which was when we switched from "Goodes' milk" in all of the stores to the big-name companies. Everyone complained for years about how the milk wasn't the same. "Did you know the guy who lived there after the Goodes passed?"

"Oh, I never knew him, I only heard many stories."

"What stories?"

"Well, that fella was a jack of all trades, you could say. He dipped his hands into just about every illegal scheme you could think of. I heard rumors he had ties to the mafia. That guy was blonde haired and blue eyed, yet supposedly Italian. Now you explain that to me, Officer. Never did understand it, but I suspect he was providing something to them. Very odd character."

I'd never heard about the owner of Patch Lane until just then. "Where is he now?" I asked.

"Oh, he left town quite a few years ago. Never did see him again. Ah well, anywho, here's some penicillin you're going to have to give to Hallie for the next five days. She has an abscess on her paw. It should open on its own, which is good. You can wrap it in warm compresses, and make sure to clean the area daily. This medication will help clear her up and fight this infection. If her paw gets worse, call my office."

Wait. What the hell? I'm going to have to give her medicine...so now I have a cat? I was more of a dog person, but I couldn't stomach the idea of dropping her off at the local shelter either. *Ugh.* On my way home, I stopped at a local mart and picked up a litter box, some cat litter, and cat food. At least cats were lower maintenance and more independent than dogs.

Once home, it didn't take long for Hallie to make herself feel welcome and curl up on my bed. I stared at her as she slept, still experiencing the feeling of familiarity. I tossed my keys on my desk, and out of the corner of my eye, I saw my mom's drawing journal. *Wait a second...* I opened it to the picture of the black cat. I stared at the page, and then at Hallie. She was nearly identical. I joined Hallie in bed, and she decided to snuggle up next to me for the night. I had to admit, it was the best I'd slept in months.

Patch Lane

Chapter 10

I should be productive before I go to work today. It was a lot easier to think about being productive than actually doing it. I rubbed my eyes and sat upright, crossing my legs. I grabbed my knees and twisted my body to the right. *Crack.* Ah, much better. I fed Hallie her breakfast and began cooking bacon and eggs. Yes, I was going to treat myself to food that didn't come out of a wrapper for once. The smell of bacon filled the air and made me crave coffee. I threw a small pot on and already began feeling productive. It's funny how caffeine is associated with productivity.

I wondered who would have more information on Patch Lane or Michelle Kline. All my thoughts came back to the same person—my dad. He was on the force back in the '90s; hell, he was on the force even back in the '80s. I also really owed him a visit since I promised I would see him after he was released from the hospital. Don't get me wrong, it certainly wasn't a chore to see my dad. He's honestly my best friend, and I wished I could see him every day, but I struggled with balancing my time off work and my chaotic schedule.

I drove over to his house, and as I pulled into the driveway, I saw the rosebush in bloom out front. The roses were such a beautiful and bright shade of red. I made a mental note to make an attempt to draw them later, even though I knew there wasn't a color that existed that would do the real color justice. The sight of roses instantly reminded me of my mom. Every time I went to my dad's, I found pieces of her everywhere, including this rosebush that she'd planted. I welcomed myself inside and was greeted with his usual bear hug. After feeding me and fueling me with his famous, super-secret coffee recipe, we sat down to catch up.

"How's your knee feeling, Dad?"

"It's less painful now than it was before the surgery, if that tells you anything."

"Oh man, I'm sorry I couldn't make it over sooner." I began to feel like the world's worst daughter when I realized how much pain he must have been in and I'd never even acknowledged it. "When did the hospital release you?"

"I've been home for almost a week now. Maggie has been over almost every day to help me out. She takes her job as big sister very seriously, you know."

"Yeah, I know. She's really the best." I'd always felt closest to my Aunt Maggie out of all my aunts and uncles. I redirected our conversation. "I'm guessing you've seen the news about the body we found on Patch Lane?"

My dad nodded his head. "Yeah. I didn't see much information on it, though. That house has been abandoned for years. Who was the body? Someone homeless?"

I shook my head. "No, it wasn't a homeless person. It was actually someone pretty important." His eyebrows raised, but he knew that if I wasn't offering more information, it was because I couldn't legally disclose the identity. The U.S. Marshals were still making the next of kin notification and wanted to work through some details of the case before telling the public the identity of Michelle Kline. "Dad, have you ever been to the house on Patch Lane?"

My dad wore a slight smile as he remembered. "Oh, wow. Yes, I have, many, many years ago."

"Really? What were you there for?"

He paused for quite a bit of time, like he was really thinking through his answer. "Well, I know I went there in the late '90s for an

ATF raid. The ATF needed a couple uniformed officers to assist them with gathering evidence for a case. I did a decent amount of help with the feds on various cases. They busted the owner of that place for distributing undocumented guns and we found them stored in a shed on the farm."

"What? I've been researching this place for over a week and I've never heard of an ATF raid."

"Well, that's because it was confidential. We never wrote a police report on the incident because it was solely documented on the federal level, and they were very good about keeping it out of the media. We didn't have space phones back then, so it was much easier to keep this under wrap."

I chuckled at my dad's reference to smart phones as space phones. "Do you know what happened to the owner? Who was he?"

"His name was...John. No, wait...Joseph, yeah Joseph. Um, Joseph Muller I believe. It was similar to Miller, but not quite Miller."

"And what happened to him?"

"Right. Well, he had an inside mole with the police department and caught wind of the raid. He flew the coop and I've never really gotten an update since then."

I began to wonder why Tim didn't tell me the history of Patch Lane. "Dad, I've been dispatched to Patch Lane several times with Tim and he never mentioned any of this. Do you know why he wouldn't tell me about it?"

"Well, Tim didn't join the department until about 1998. This all happened around 1997, about a year before he joined the force." My dad took a sip of his coffee and added, "You know Sarah, you should really be spending your free time doing normal twenty-five-year-old things like going bowling or something fun with your friends. Or, of course, you can spend your free time relaxing with your old man. Regardless, you shouldn't be spending every waking minute investigating."

Despite his own advice, my dad began to ask me questions about my calls to Patch Lane. It was hard to answer him fully because I was distracted by my eagerness to continue investigating and following up on Michelle Kline's case. I preferred having my questions answered rather than be the one answering questions. I ended up making a dash to the front door and told my dad I had to get going because of Hallie. I quickly explained to him how I had taken in a stray who was still healing.

Speaking of being eager for answers, I realized that I hadn't heard back from the Pennsylvania State Police Forensic Lab yet, so from the car, I called them to get an update on what was written on the back of the receipt I found in Michelle's pocket. A receptionist answered the phone, "Pennsylvania State Forensic Department."

"Hello, this is Officer Hastings following up on the Patch Lane case. I wanted to check the status of my evidence." I pulled out my notebook and read the case number to the receptionist.

"Hold on, let me check." After about one minute went by, she got back on the phone. "Hi, I just checked, and I see your evidence is still being processed. Looks like you dropped it off this week and we're pretty backlogged right now. I suspect we should have it done within the next couple days."

I headed home and started the ritualistic process of getting ready for the night's shift. Only one shift away from my weekend. Most people hate Mondays, but since they were my version of Friday, I'd come to love them.

Chapter 11

We hit the road and the night started out fairly slow. Peterson and I tucked our cruisers behind one of the elementary schools and leaned against our hoods while I sipped on my coffee and he spat into an empty soda can.

"Your wife must find that so attractive," I commented as he was mid-spit.

He half-laughed and responded, "Yeah right, like her smoking is that much better."

Then, I made the mistake of admitting out loud, "It's been pretty quiet so far."

Peterson looked at me out of the corner of his eye after I said the forbidden word—quiet. It was a curse in this line of work; as soon as someone said "quiet," a shitstorm headed their way. It was only a matter of minutes before Dispatch got on the radio.

"Dispatch to any CIT officer on shift."

That would be me. I'd attended the Crisis Intervention Team training, a nationwide training for law enforcement officers on how to interact with individuals who have a mental illness, autism, or various other developmental disabilities and illnesses. We only had three patrol officers who'd gone through this CIT training. When I'd found out about it, I made a formal proposal to Chief Fox explaining why I wanted to attend the training and how my Psychology degree would make me a prime candidate. Surprisingly, he agreed. I later learned that Chief Fox had used this opportunity as a platform at the next city council meeting to commend himself on outsourcing new trainings to better serve the community.

I keyed my radio, "1034, I am CIT trained. Go ahead."

"1034, we have a caller who is requesting to speak with an officer because her neighbor won't stop watching her. When the call taker asked who her neighbor was, she said that her neighbor was a tree. She went on to say that he's been watching her through the wires in her house."

I knew I was going to have my hands full for a while talking to this caller and trying to convince her to go back on her medications. Dispatch sent me the address, and I had to use my GPS to help me get there, as Chip Lane was one of the very few roads in Amber Forest that I had not heard of before. I plugged the address into my GPS and finally understood why I had never heard of it. The caller's home was the sole house on a private lane. I couldn't help but notice that the Patch Lane farm sat to the rear of the caller's property.

"Officer! Over here!"

I didn't see anyone at the front door, so I followed the gritty, smoker's voice to the side of the old farmhouse. An older woman was sitting on her side porch in her nightgown, puffing away at a cigarette. By the looks of her wrinkles and the sound of her voice, this woman must have been smoking a pack a day for over forty years. "Hi ma'am, I'm Officer Hastings."

"Thank you for coming out! I have been so busy cleaning this house, listening to the words, and organizing the information. They won't shut the hell up. I told them a hundred times before in school I'm not interested."

Disorganized speech…red flag for mental illness. I needed to get her to calm down since she was showing signs of a manic phase. "Ma'am, I understand that you are very concerned. I'm sorry, but I never caught your name. What is your name?"

She took a long puff of her cigarette, and as she blew out the smoke, she answered, "Lu. Short for Lulu like my mother used to call me. She called me like the pigs to come get food, 'LULU BELL!'"

"It's nice to meet you, Lu. It's awfully late, can you tell me why you called the police tonight?"

"Oh, I know it's late. I do my sleeping during the day when they watch me. I like to sit out on my porch at night to make it harder. I called the police because the tree is watching me. I see him all the time through my window. He's not my tree though, he's the neighbor's. I just want him to stop. I yell at him to stop it and go back home but he's always there, especially at night."

I nodded my head as she talked to "make excellent use of my active listening skills," as my CIT instructor had hammered into us. I wanted to earn her trust and show sympathy as I prepared to ask her the one question that always tended to elicit a response. "Lu, are you currently prescribed any medications?"

"Ah, hell with medication. It makes me feel all blah, you know? Just blah. You're not my doctor, you can't tell me how to diagnose my pills and tell me what I taste."

Lu was starting to get worked up, and I needed to find a solution to help her settle as well as prevent her from calling the cops repeatedly in the future. Due to officers merely placing a band-aid over these issues and not taking the time to find long-term solutions, we had our fair share of mentally ill residents call us on a nightly basis. One example that I always thought about was when Tim made a hat out of foil and told a guy that if he wore the hat, the FBI would not be able to hear his thoughts. Tim honestly thought he was helping the guy by doing that, but after my training I explained to him that he was only hurting the guy by feeding into his delusions.

I started walking towards Lu's front door. "Lu, do you mind if I take a look around inside?"

Lu opened her pack of cigarettes and took another out. She waved her hand in the air. "Yeah, yeah, go ahead. Do whatever you want."

I headed towards the bathroom to look for any medications. I walked through the family room and into the short hallway. There were only two doors in the hallway, and I could tell the one on the left was a closet door. I opened the other to find a pink tiled bathroom with a rusting medicine cabinet hanging over the sink. Inside I found some band-aids, soap, and cotton swabs.

Before I headed upstairs to check if there was another bathroom, I decided to look in the kitchen. As I walked through the family room, I glanced out the window and saw Lu was still sitting on the side porch, smoking away like a chimney. Once in the kitchen, I opened the cabinets on both sides of the sink and slowly worked my way outward. I finally found a small corner cabinet that had approximately a dozen bottles of various medications. There was one labeled Olanzapine and I pulled it out. It was last refilled nearly six months ago for sixty pills and had instructions to take one pill once a day.

I saw the doctor's name and phone number on the top corner of the label and called her office. Not surprisingly, I got her voicemail since it was the middle of the night. I left a message for the doctor to give me a call back regarding her patient, Lu. I knew that her doctor was not going to be able to give me any information about Lu, but I intended to tell her doctor about my interaction with her and simply advise her that she was no longer taking her medications.

I put the bottle back in the cabinet and headed back outside to talk to Lu. CIT training had taught me that it was common for people's delusions to have bits of truth to them. I thought that there could possibly be an owl or another animal that regularly sat in her tree and annoyed her. Without being there myself, I couldn't exactly be sure what was upsetting Lu.

"Alright, Lu, I just called your doctor and hopefully will hear from her tomorrow. I called her because I'm concerned that your current emotional state is a result of not taking your medications."

Lu finished her cigarette and was shaking her head back and forth. "No, no, no, I'm fine."

I wasn't surprised that Lu had been smoking the entire time, since it was common for people with a mental illness to attempt to self-medicate with alcohol, tobacco, or other recreational drugs. "Well, I can tell you're very agitated by the number of cigarettes you've smoked since I arrived."

Lu admitted, "Yeah, I'm a little agitated you could say."

"Do you think you could at least stop by Dr. Boyd's office tomorrow? I'm worried about you, and it would make me feel better to know that you at least spoke to Dr. Boyd."

Lu agreed to stop by her doctor's office the next day, so I said my goodbyes and headed on my way.

Patch Lane

Chapter 12

It felt like I had worked two weeks straight without a weekend, since I'd spent my last days off researching Michelle Kline's case. Not this time. Thanks to my dad pointing out my lack of social life, I decided I was going to let myself have some fun those next two days.

"GIRL. Where is your wine at?" Christie always seemed to know how to distract me from work. We'd been best friends since middle school, and even if I fell off the face of the earth for several weeks, we acted like not a day had gone by since we last saw each other.

"Are we in a red or white mood?"

Christie crinkled her nose as she thought, finally settling on her decision. "Red. Red goes well with popcorn and scary movies!"

I grabbed my finest fifteen-dollar bottle of merlot and poured two glasses. Christie made her way to the couch and Hallie followed suit.

Christie petted her and asked, "Where did you say you got Hallie from?"

"I actually don't think I told you yet. I found her at the Patch Lane house."

Christie's eyes widened and she stopped petting Hallie. "You mean to tell me this cat came from the Werner Farm?"

"Yeah...why?"

"Damn. You probably just brought back a haunted cat or something. Haven't you heard the stories about that place? Granted she's, like, the cutest haunted cat ever. But still."

I rolled my eyes at Christie and assured her that Hallie was not haunted. I grabbed one of the DVDs that Christie had brought over and popped it into my DVD player. We had our horror movie marathon, and for the first time in days, I didn't think about Michelle Kline. Christie slept over on my couch, since she knew I would never let her drive after having more than two glasses of wine. It was nice to have company and give the silence in my apartment a break.

"SARAH!" I woke up to Christie yelling my name.

I jumped out of bed and ran into the family room. I'm not sure if it was Christie's yelling or my sudden movement, but poor Hallie nearly fell right off the bed. "What's going on? What's the problem?" I stood in the middle of my family room, both hands above my waist, ready to go.

Christie giggled at the site of my tactical stance in nothing but my underwear and a tank top. "Oh Sarah, if only you could see what you look like right now. I'm sorry, I didn't mean to startle you. I opened your cabinet and saw that you only had regular coffee, even though I asked you THREE TIMES since the last time I was here to make sure you got me decaf."

Christie couldn't have caffeine because she was sensitive to it. One time we went to the local coffee shop and Christie ordered hot chocolate, since she was craving it more than a latte or coffee. After she'd finished her hot chocolate, she was grabbing at her chest telling me she thought she was having a heart attack. After a trip to the emergency room, Christie and I both learned that some places actually put caffeine in their hot chocolate.

My eyebrows lowered and I glared at her. "I bought you decaf and it's still in the goddamn bag on the kitchen counter. We certainly don't want you to have another heart attack, now do we?"

Christie walked over to the counter and opened the grocery bag to find her decaf coffee. "Oh shush," she embarrassedly laughed. "Thank you, Sarah…you're the best!"

I wasn't thrilled by my wake-up call, but we both got a good laugh about it later. We were slow to get around, but eventually we got ourselves together and headed out for a fun girls' lunch.

We each ordered fishbowl-sized margaritas and, after a brief contemplation between fajitas or burritos, we agreed to split an order of chicken fajitas. As I was inhaling the chips and salsa, Christie started asking me about Patch Lane.

"So, you said you're working the Patch Lane case, right?"

"Yeah, I can't really say too much about it, though."

Christie held her hand up to show she understood. "I know, I know, I'm not going to ask you about the case. I want to know about the *house*."

I finished chewing my chip with a massive heap of salsa. "What do you mean?"

"Well, like, is it really haunted? How creepy was it? I remember going there once in high school when I dated Dave because we thought it would be cool to take pictures and look for ghosts." Christie had always been into the supernatural; she was the reason I got into horror movies.

I debated whether to tell her about the person I saw run from the kitchen and disappear. "Yeah, I would definitely say that place is creepy. I'm not too sure I would say I saw any ghosts there, though. You and Dave find anything during your, uh, ghost hunting expedition?"

"Oh my god, yeah we did! We took pictures of the house and also in the woods around it to see if we could capture some orbs or whatever. Anyway, we got a picture of a guy walking through the woods. It was clear as day, you could see his legs, his arms, his head, everything. I saw it on my camera as soon as I took the picture, but when I looked up, he wasn't there. It's like he literally vanished into thin air."

Christie tended to have an overactive imagination, so I didn't think too much into what she said. People don't just vanish into thin air. But then again, that's the only way I could explain what happened to the shadowy figure I saw. We finished our lunches and I gave her a huge hug as we said goodbye.

"I really needed this girls' time. Thank you." I gave Christie an extra squeeze before releasing her.

Christie waved as she got into her car and I headed back towards mine.

I was stopped at a red light a block away when I started to think what I should do with the rest of my free day. *Hmm, maybe my dad would be up for having dinner together. I feel bad I kinda ran out on him last time.* As I turned into his driveway, I recognized Tim's truck. It wasn't much of a surprise to see him there, since he and my dad were good friends and Tim had the same days off as me. My dad wrapped his arms around me and was happy for the surprise visit. Tim gave me a nod of the head, smiled, and asked, "How's it going?"

"Hey! I'm really glad you guys are both here. I wanted to ask you two about Patch Lane."

Tim chimed in, "Jesus, see what I'm talking about? Your girl is obsessed with this case now. Chip off the old block, am I right?"

My dad laughed, "Oh I remember those days of obsessing over cases...I gotta say, retirement has treated me well."

I welcomed myself back into the conversation, "Okay, well, maybe there's a reason to be obsessed. I talked to some U.S. Marshals and found out our Jane Doe was actually in the Witness Protection Program." I added, "Tim, I also wanted to ask you about the 911 hang ups you used to respond to back when you were a rookie. What else do you remember about the tenant?"

Tim thought for a moment and replied, "Well, I basically told you everything I remember. She was certainly a young and pretty girl. I would suspect she was maybe around twenty years old, if that. Just had that baby face, ya know? Anyways, she was very curious about the house and the locked door in the basement. Most people hated when the cops showed up, but she always seemed...I don't know, relieved?

She would mention how big that house was and how she always felt like someone was watching her. Even the tenants after her made similar comments about feeling like someone was watching them. I always chalked it up to being the history of that Werner Farm, ya know?"

"You met other tenants too, then? How?"

"We kept getting 911 hang up calls for that house for quite a few years. They basically stopped for the most part when the house became abandoned."

"Tim, is there any chance that the woman we found in that basement was the same girl that lived there twenty years ago?"

"I don't know why it would be. I always thought she moved somewhere else, because right after she left a new tenant came in. I guess I don't know exactly what happened to her..." Tim trailed off.

"Do you remember her name?"

"Oh god, I'm awful with names. I'll never forget a face, but I can't remember names. You know that. That's why I always write every person's name down that we interview. I can't even check anywhere since I never took a report for checking her house."

"Could her name have been Michelle Kline?"

"Honestly, I don't know. It could have, but I have no idea. It was twenty years ago."

My dad took long, rapid puffs of his cigar. It almost seemed like he felt uncomfortable, which wasn't normal since Tim and I were the two people closest to him. I suspected that I might have intruded on their guy time, so I made my visit brief and left the two of them back to it.

My stomach started to growl. A hoagie sounded damn good right about then, so I stopped on my way home for a Philly cheesesteak hoagie and ended up sharing most of my cheese with Hallie.

Patch Lane

68

Chapter 13

"Hi, this is Matt Sloan, one of the Deputy Marshals you spoke with last week."

For some reason, I was expecting it to be Sergeant Oakley on the phone. Why would I think that? I pulled the phone away from my ear and looked at the incoming caller ID. It was my station's phone number. "Oh. Hi, Matt. Sorry, I wasn't expecting you when I saw my station was calling." I grabbed the water off my nightstand and took a swig to help soothe my morning voice.

"Sorry if I woke you. Jackson and I checked out that old root cellar you and your partner found last week. We were hoping you could walk us through exactly how you found it and tell us what you touched and moved."

"Oh, yeah, I wrote it all down in my report but I'm happy to come by and go over the scene with you in greater detail."

"Great! Thanks so much. I'm already at the station so I'll let Chief Fox know you're going to come in early today."

"Sounds good, see you soon."

Hallie started batting at my phone as I said goodbye. "Alright, alright, I'll get up." I gave Hallie a few scratches to her right cheek before getting out of bed.

I got to the station and saw that Matt was talking to Chief Fox. I walked up behind Matt and said, "Hey, Deputy. I'm here whenever you're ready to go."

Matt turned around and smiled. "Okay, great!" He turned back to Chief Fox and finished up his conversation. "It was a pleasure talking to you, sir. Thanks for all the help!"

I followed Matt outside to his car but didn't see Deputy Jackson anywhere. "Is Deputy Jackson coming with us?" I asked.

Matt opened the driver side door and responded, "He was going to, but he got a call from his wife back home in Pittsburgh this morning. She was having contractions and thought she might go into labor, so he got a rental and hit the road."

"Oh wow, I didn't realize he had a wife who was expecting."

"Yeah, well, we try not to talk about our personal lives too much."

"Well, I hope you don't have an expecting wife back home for the sake of this case, then." *Why did I just say that?* I could be so awkward sometimes. I tried to hide my embarrassment and began to fiddle with my vest.

Matt gently laughed and responded, "Oh no, no wife back home for me."

I needed to quickly redirect the conversation. "So, do you think Jackson will come back for the case?"

"I told him I would let him know if I needed him to head back over here. It's not that far of a drive."

As Matt began driving, I realized the car we were in was a Subaru Forester. It had all the normal police equipment like any unmarked vehicle, but I was used to seeing a Ford or Dodge. I commented, "A Subaru police vehicle? I've never seen that before."

"Oh yeah, we have a few vehicles in our fleet that are very inconspicuous. It helps when we do surveillance details."

"Interesting. So, since Michelle Kline was in WITSEC, does that mean that her murder is technically your investigation?"

Matt quickly glanced at me, then took his eyes back to the road. "Actually, no. This is the FBI's case, but we have a task force that consists of FBI, ATF, and U.S. Marshals. I think I briefly mentioned that to you the first time we met. Sorry I didn't get to explain it further. The FBI supervisor assigned to this case is back in Pittsburgh handling the administrative work. They sent me out to do the field work. I hope you don't mind working together on this case."

Before I realized it, Matt had pulled onto the gravel lane and I could see the old farmhouse. I forgot how different this place looked in the daylight. It was less creepy, but sadder. I could envision this farm as having been beautiful at one point, like how Dr. Demeyers explained it.

I walked Matt through exactly how Tim and I came across the root cellar and the path that we took. I showed him everywhere I could remember touching, and we slowly worked our way back outside. I saw the network interface device box on the side of the house and decided to tell Matt about my theory of the 911 hang ups.

"You know how I kept getting dispatched here because of 911 hang ups coming from this house?"

"Yeah." Matt's gaze was glued to the ground, trying not to get his nice shoes covered in mud as we walked through the overgrown grass.

"Well, don't you find that odd considering there's no electricity to this house? There's not even a phone inside, I checked."

Matt took his eyes off his shoes and looked at me. "Sarah, I find this entire damn case odd."

"I learned the other day that there are these phone boxes attached to houses that connect old landline telephones to the central system. You can actually plug a phone into one of these boxes and make calls from them that show up as coming from one of the addresses that are connected to the box."

Matt squinted his eyes as he tried to figure out where I was going with this. "Okay...so do you think someone called from a phone box around here?"

"I don't know, it's just a theory I have. I found one here the other day. It's over there." I pointed to the side of the old farmhouse.

Matt glanced towards the house and looked back to meet my eyes. "Show me."

We walked to the phone box and I opened the front panel to show Matt the innards of the box. I relayed everything to him that Scooter had explained to me. Matt looked just as surprised as I had when I learned about these boxes, which made sense because he appeared to be only a couple years older than me.

"That is some weird shit," Matt said as he shook his head. He asked, "Do you have any inclination as to who would have made the phone calls?"

"I don't have any leads. I'm not even positive that's how they did it, but it's a theory."

I closed the panel door. Matt suggested that we take a walk through the acreage and along the tree line, to scope out the land and look for anything else suspicious. We made our way through the overgrown fields and towards the woods.

Matt changed our conversation to a lighter tone. "So, what is there to do for fun in Amber Forest, anyway?"

"If you ask my dad, he'll tell you bowling. But honestly, there isn't much to do here except drink. That's why we have so many DUI problems and underage drinking citations."

"Ah yes, I remember those d—" before Matt could finish his sentence, he was halfway to the ground.

My reflexes kicked in, and before I realized what was happening, I had both of my arms under Matt's and I was holding his upper body nearly six inches off the ground. I slowly brought him to his knees, then to his feet. So much for keeping his nice shoes clean.

Matt brushed off his pant legs and said, "Thank you. I thought I was going to eat dirt for a second. I have no idea what the hell I tripped on."

We looked around the ground and it felt like déjà vu. There was another root cellar door sticking up from the ground. "Jesus Christ, there's another root cellar!" I exclaimed.

Matt's mouth fell open in astonishment and he knelt to get a better look. To our surprise, the root cellar was somewhat camouflaged with brush but not completely overgrown. There was a padlock on the door and before I could ask how to get it open, Matt pulled out a lock pick set. I began to think that he was the only person more prepared than me. He worked on the lock for about a minute before I heard the satisfying *pop*. We opened the root cellar door with ease, and I shined my flashlight into the dark room. Matt walked down first. *He is clearly more of a gentleman than Tim.* When we both reached the bottom step, I shined my light wall to wall. The cellar was filled with guns.

I walked up to one of the guns and reached up to take it off the wall. Matt yelled, "Don't touch it!"

I stopped myself. "You're right. Hold on, I should have gloves somewhere." I reached around my back to a pouch on my duty belt where I always kept spare sets of latex gloves. They came in handy since I frequently had to process my own crime scenes. I took one pair out for myself and handed a second pair to Matt.

Matt squeezed his hands into the gloves. "Geeze, you have tiny hands."

"That may be so, but I bet they could do twice the damage of yours," I replied and smirked.

"Damn, alright."

I put on my gloves and picked up one of the AR-15s hanging on the wall. There had to be over a dozen of the exact same gun. I held it at eye level while Matt shined my flashlight onto the weapon. I looked it over, turning it in my hands. There wasn't a serial number on this gun.

The ATF eventually arrived to process the scene. Thanks to Matt's federal connections, he was able to get two local ATF agents on site within forty-five minutes, and eventually more joined from Pittsburgh.

The sun was about to set, so they had to move fast if they didn't want to end up collecting evidence in pitch blackness.

I asked one of the ATF agents, "So, what's the deal with all of these guns with missing serial numbers? Do you think they were used in crimes? How old are they?"

He responded, "They look pretty new actually. If you look closely, you can see that there were once serial numbers on the guns, but they were filed down. Whoever did these filings was meticulous. This is some of the most impressive work we've seen in a while. None of these guns appear to have ever been fired before. I would guess that this guy was selling these undocumented guns to criminals. I was looking through our records for this address and saw that we did a raid here over twenty years ago. Doubtful it's the same guy since there's still an active warrant out for him, Joseph Muller, but you never know. Some people are just that stupid that they stick around."

Matt offered to treat me to a drink after we left the scene in ATF's control. I quickly ran home so I could change and not have to wear a black t-shirt and BDUs. I threw on some jeans, a white blouse, and my favorite brown leather jacket. I met him at the local watering hole for Amber Forest townies—Luna's—and ordered my usual IPA while Matt opted for a neat whiskey. When he ordered his drink, I gave him a nod of approval. I appreciate a man who could drink his liquor neat.

"Nice jacket," Matt said as he gave me his own nod of approval.

We bullshitted about our day and I slowly worked my way towards asking him about Michelle Kline. Matt quickly clammed up and responded, "I really can't discuss any details about her. We did make next of kin notification—her aunt, who's going to notify Michelle's son. They both live down in Maryland and I made sure to send a deputy directly to their home. All I can tell you is that she was a witness to Joseph Muller's gun running ring and he wanted her dead. After seeing all those guns in that root cellar today, it makes me wonder if there are additional root cellars on that 100-acre farm with more guns. And why is he still using that farm? We all thought he would be long gone by now. But now, I'm beginning to think Muller is still around and he's the one who killed Michelle." He added, "And you wanna know something else? I didn't know what the hell a root cellar was until this case. I'm a concrete Pittsburgh boy." He took another sip of his whiskey. "Amber Forest is like another country compared to Pittsburgh."

Maybe I can trust this guy. He seems pretty down to earth. I decided to tell him about my issues at the Medical Examiner's office. "Did you notice anything suspicious about Michelle's autopsy report?" I asked.

"Yeah. It was a shitty job. My boss really went at it with your Chief Medical Examiner. I had to listen to the lead FBI agent bitch for almost twenty minutes about how annoying it is to work with small towns. No offense."

"None taken," I lied.

"Anyway, he told me to look into the guy. I interviewed him and it turns out he was threatened into not performing the autopsy."

"What? By who?" I stopped drinking and was entirely focused on Matt's information.

"We don't know yet. I'm putting my money on Joseph or one of his connections. Whoever it was had emailed him a photograph of his family with a letter saying they'd be killed if he performed an autopsy on Michelle Kline. By the time we figured all this out, her body had already been cremated." Matt took another sip of his drink. "I probably shouldn't be telling you all of these details. Ah, hell with it."

I didn't want to push him into specifics that could cost him his job, so I stopped asking about Michelle Kline. After finishing my second beer, I waved to the bartender for my check.

I finally got home and began wondering what next steps we should take to catch Joseph Muller. It was beginning to look like he'd never left his farm. Not to mention, he had ample motive to want Michelle dead. I knew I had to go into work the next day, so I did my best to shut my brain off with a hot shower, a glass of wine, and one of my favorite horror movies.

Chapter 14

Roll call was pretty short and sweet since we were getting busy and Sergeant Oakley wanted bodies on the road as soon as possible. I was in the middle of a conversation when Dispatch interrupted.

"Dispatch to 1034."

"1034, go ahead."

"Are you able to respond to a 911 hang up?"

"Affirmative. What's the address?"

"1207 Cranberry Road."

I sighed with relief that Dispatch didn't say Patch Lane. "Show me en route."

I racked my cruiser and headed towards the house. I turned down the gravel road, kicking up dust in my Taurus's path. I stopped a few yards away from the old log cabin and approached quietly. To my surprise, there was an elderly woman through the window, sitting in her floral chair and watching television. I didn't see anyone else in the house, so I approached and knocked. "Officer Hastings with the Amber Forest Police Department. Please come to the front door!"

The woman slowly raised herself from the chair and took hold of her walker. She came to the front door and greeted me, "Hello there, Officer. Is there something wrong?"

"Ma'am, is everything alright? We received a 911 hang up from this residence."

She responded, "Oh yes, everything is just fine here, Officer. It was probably just my husband."

Growing concerned, I instantly asked, "Where is your husband? I need to go check to make sure he's alright, then."

She shrugged her shoulders and pointed towards the fireplace. "He's right there, Officer."

I looked to where she was pointing, but nobody was there. "Ma'am, I don't see your husband. Can you please tell me what room he is in?"

She slowly walked over to the fireplace mantel and pointed to the center. "He's here, Officer." She was pointing to an urn.

"Oh, I see him now. I'm so sorry for your loss." I wasn't sure what her response was going to be, but I knew it was important to not mislead her by pretending he was still alive.

"Yes, why, thank you. Saying sorry is such an odd tradition, don't you think? I mean, I know you aren't the reason he's dead. Anywho, I'm sorry that you came out for that. Ever since Samuel passed a few months ago he's been messing with the wires. He turns the lights on and off and I keep getting phone calls from family members saying they are returning my call, but I never called them. It's always nice for me since I get to talk to them and catch up on current events in their lives. I guess it's his way of letting me know he's still here with me and checking in on me."

I didn't really believe in the paranormal, but the way she talked about her husband's ghost so casually gave me chills. I gave the woman a heartfelt smile and reached out my hand. "I'm sorry I didn't get to formally introduce myself. I'm Sarah Hastings. Please feel free to call me Sarah."

"Oh. Hi, Sarah, I'm Rose. It is very nice to meet you. Again, I'm sorry you got called out here for nothing, I'm sure you have much more important places to be."

"No, it's quite alright. This is an important call to me. However, per my department's protocol, I need to check your home to make sure that there isn't anyone else in here who could have made the call. Is that alright?"

"Yes, of course. I understand. I'll just sit out here. I've been home all day, though. There certainly isn't anyone here but me." She settled back into her chair and continued watching her television as if I wasn't even there.

Starting with the first floor, I cleared the kitchen, then the family room, and made my way to the master bedroom. I made sure to check every closet and every place a person could hide.

First floor was clear, so I headed to the basement. There was an old work bench covered in different machines and tools used for loading ammunition. I knew these items quite well since it was a hobby my dad had for years. Everything was covered in dust; it looked as though loading ammunition was an old hobby of Samuel's. I could see he had an assortment of empty shells lined up on a tray as if he was preparing to load them. He had a very fine antique loading press that I knew would make my dad jealous. I began to wonder if Rose knew the value of these antiques she had sitting in her basement. As my eyes trailed down his work bench, I was impressed with his organization and tidiness. His ammunition and tools were all set up, ready for him to return to work at any moment. I glanced towards the corner to the cellar door, where his jacket hung on a single hook. I didn't even know Samuel, but I began to empathize with Rose and felt as though he'd never left.

I made my way to the laundry room, where I noticed an old dehumidifier sitting in the corner. It caught my eye since it had a wood paneling pattern on the plastic cover, much like the old minivan my dad used to have in the early '90s. I also noticed it didn't have a hose hooked up to a drain; it was the kind that had a bucket which needed to be emptied on a regular basis. I remembered complaining once about how heavy my dad's dehumidifier bucket was when I was watching his house while he was away. I couldn't imagine how Rose emptied that thing on a regular basis. She was one tough lady.

I finally headed back upstairs after clearing the basement, wedging my duty belt between the stair railing and the chairlift that Rose had installed. I walked through the family room to another set of stairs leading to a second-floor loft. I cautiously walked upstairs and opened the door to the loft bedroom.

I could smell the stale air from a room that clearly had not been used in years. I checked the closet and under the bed. Right as I went to leave, I noticed a small cubby door in the corner behind the door. I had to check anywhere that a person could possibly hide, so I opened the cubby door with my left hand, while keeping my right resting on my gun. The storage space was pitch black. I grabbed my flashlight and shined it into the darkness. The cubby space was nearly empty except for an outdated lamp, a wooden sled, and an old trunk with brass locks. When I looked at the trunk, every hair on the back of my neck stood up and goosebumps covered my arms. My intuition had steered me right so far, so I'd learned to follow it.

I slowly crawled through the cubby, making my way towards the trunk. I opened the lid and found it was full of various items; no person hiding in it. I released an audible sigh of relief. I decided to drag the trunk out of the cubby, especially since I knew Rose was unable to walk up those stairs and I thought maybe this would be something she would like to know about. I hollered over the loft railing, "Rose, there's an old trunk in this cubby hole. Did you know that was up here?"

Rose replied, "What? What trunk?"

I carried it downstairs to let her look through it. I set it down at her feet and opened it. I could see it much clearer now that we were in the light. There were old newspaper clippings, photographs, and clothing. One photograph in particular caught Rose's eye. She leaned over and picked it up, caressing the edges. She began to cry and my immediate response was to comfort her. "Rose, I'm so sorry. What's wrong?"

She sat and wept for a few moments. When she was able to answer, she whispered, "It's a photograph of my granddaughter. I not only lost her once, I lost her twice. Sometimes the pain is just too much to bear."

"What do you mean you lost her twice?"

Rose responded, "Don't you know, honey? My granddaughter was Michelle Kline, the woman the police found in the Patch Lane house."

I couldn't control my facial muscles as my jaw dropped. "Wait, Michelle Kline was your granddaughter?" I knew I was repeating what she'd just said, but it was a shocking detail and difficult to process.

"Yes, you look surprised. Were you one of the officers who found her?"

"Oh Rose, yes I was. I am so sorry for your loss. I guess I always thought she was more of a transient. I had no idea that she had family left in the area."

"Well, I think I'm the only family left here. Michelle's son went to live with our other daughter down in Maryland twenty years ago after we believed she died."

I knew Michelle's children were in Maryland, because Matt mentioned it when explaining they made notification to Michelle's next of kin. I had so many questions for Rose but tried to pace myself. I started by asking, "What was your relationship with Michelle like?"

"She was less like a granddaughter and more like a daughter to me. I love Michelle's mother very much. She is my daughter after all, but she has her flaws. She had a newfound religious awakening when she married Michelle's father. If you ask me, I'd say her awakening was a little too extreme. Naturally, when Michelle came home and told them she was pregnant and going to be raising a child alone, they did not react kindly. They kicked her out of their house. I don't think it was even six months before they ended up moving out West and took Samantha, Michelle's younger sister. I was so upset to see my family leave, but Kathy said they had to move to be closer to Alan's family." Rose sighed,

"I knew Kathy chose Alan over us a long time ago. I don't know why it surprised me when she moved. It was a few years later that our other daughter, Regina, moved to Maryland for a job, then it was only me and Samuel left in Amber Forest."

I was losing track of all the new names, so I asked, "Alan?"

"Yes, Michelle's father."

"Oh, sorry. So, what did Michelle do when they kicked her out?"

"She had nowhere to go. Samuel and I took her in and helped her through her pregnancy. Oh God, and then the accident happened."

"What accident?"

"Michelle was driving down the road to work, she was a waitress, and got hit head-on by a drunk driver. She was seven months pregnant and we didn't know if either of them was going to make it. I think that night took years off my life."

I cringed as the thought of the accident ran through my mind, reminding me of the scene only two weeks earlier. "That's so terrifying."

"Yes, it was," Rose replied. "As I'm sure you can figure out, they both survived. Michelle suffered a severe brain injury and the doctors had to perform an emergency Caesarean section. Luckily, with therapy and the right doctors, she was able to make a full recovery."

I was dying to know how Michelle ended up at Patch Lane. "And when did she move out of your home?"

"Oh, let's see...probably about ten months after the accident. I know it wasn't a full year yet. She ended up starting her own business and made more than twice what she was making as a waitress."

Being that Amber Forest is such a small town, everyone knows all the local business owners. I was surprised to hear Michelle had started her own business, since I had never heard of her before this case. I asked, "What business did she start?"

Rose's eyes widened and she inhaled deeply, "Well, now, that's an interesting story that might take us a while."

I was so engrossed in Rose's information, I leaned in closer. "I have time, Rose."

"Alright. Well, after Michelle's accident she didn't feel the same. She started experiencing…strange things that no one could explain."

I wasn't sure where Rose was going with this, so I asked, "Like medically?"

"No, not like that. She started having thoughts, memory-like thoughts, that weren't real memories and had never happened to her. She would be confused about why she randomly had a thought, then within a day's notice her vision would come true."

This conversation was not going where I thought it would, but I was absolutely intrigued.

I could tell that Rose felt embarrassed as she continued, "I know how this must all sound. If it weren't for seeing it with my own eyes, I wouldn't have believed it either."

I took the bait and asked, "What exactly did you see?"

"I'll never forget her first vision. We were all in the family room playing cards and unwinding since she had just gotten home from work. Out of nowhere, she started crying. At first, I thought it was her hormones, since it wasn't long after Ryan was born. She said she didn't know why she was crying. But quickly, she started rocking back and forth in her seat. She kept repeating, 'No, no, no, this isn't happening. This isn't real.' Even I started crying at the sight of her. Samuel had no idea whether he should console her or sit back. He just stared in disbelief. I held her for nearly twenty minutes. When she could finally speak, she started saying that someone she loved was dead. I assured her that everyone was okay, but she couldn't stop saying 'Someone's dead.'"

The goosebumps which had appeared upon finding the trunk had found their way back onto my arms. "So, what happened?"

"We finally got her calmed down and put her to bed. It wasn't even 7:00 a.m. when we woke up to the phone ringing. Samuel answered and

I'll never forget his face. I had never seen as much pain in his eyes as that very moment." Rose pulled out a tissue from her sleeve and wiped her nose. She continued, "Samuel put the phone down and grabbed my hand. I knew something was wrong. He told me Samantha, Michelle's sister, overdosed that night."

I had no words, no response. Suddenly everything around me felt more vivid. The rain outside sounded like it was knocking on the window to come inside. I hadn't even noticed it was raining until right then. I stared at Rose's face and could see every line on her forehead, every wrinkle on her cheek. I noticed my breathing slowed. I didn't even believe in this stuff, but I felt almost frozen in time as I absorbed everything Rose was telling me.

Rose took a sip from her glass of water and didn't let the silence bother her. She continued, "And ever since that day, Michelle's visions only got clearer and more precise. Her gift really changed her life when we were walking through the park one evening. Michelle had felt a heaviness on her chest that she couldn't shake. I was concerned she was having a heart attack because of how she was acting. She had stopped walking and kept grabbing at her chest. Her breathing was so heavy, but she somehow knew that what she was experiencing wasn't medical and said she was feeling a spirit connecting to her." Rose closed her eyes and relived the moment. "Oh, Michelle had me so worried. I held onto her and after a few minutes passed, she opened her eyes and began crying hysterically. Michelle told me a little girl was buried there. Right there in the park! Michelle would not let it go and we eventually had to call the police out. There was a nice officer working that evening who listened to every word Michelle told him. I mean, he really, truly listened. You know what, I think he had something happen in his own life that made him a believer long before we called him. Anywho, he decided to go get a shovel and he started digging on his own, right there in front of us, before calling for backup. Given the circumstances, he thought it would be better to have something more concrete before calling for backup. It only took him about fifteen minutes before he eventually found a trash bag. Oh my, I remember my own breathing stopped when I heard his shovel against plastic. The officer stopped digging and didn't even open the bag before he called for additional officers and started wrapping police tape around the park."

I felt like a child during story time. I couldn't stop asking questions. "So, was there a body? What was in the bag?"

Rose exhaled deeply, "Oh yes, there was a body of a young girl. That's a sight I'll never forget. The police questioned Michelle, but it didn't take them long before they ruled her out as a suspect. Once she was ruled out, the Amber Forest Police Department realized that Michelle's gift was real and slowly started using her for help with other cases."

"Like, a psychic detective?"

Rose shrugged. "I suppose it was something like that. It's not as if she reported to work every day or all the cops knew who she was. She only responded to the chief back then, a really nice guy who died a few years back from lung cancer. Anyway, she was kind of like a silent partner to their investigations."

I tried to draw all the pieces of information together to figure out how it could possibly relate to my case. I asked, "How did Michelle eventually end up living at Patch Lane?"

"Samuel and I didn't want Michelle to move out. We were concerned for her and Ryan's safety and we really loved having them here, but Michelle felt it was important to be an independent mother and started searching for a safe but affordable home. She looked mostly in this area so we could still help with watching Ryan. One day, Michelle was at the corner store and saw a paper taped to the bulletin board for a house for rent. It was surprisingly affordable and not far from our cabin, so she left and drove straight to the house on Patch Lane to check it out. She was immediately drawn to the house, like a moth to a flame. As soon as she got home, she called the number on the paper and said she would take it. Imagine my surprise when I got home that evening and she told me she was moving into the old Werner farmhouse on Patch Lane. Everyone around here knew the stories of that old farm, but somehow those stories never got to Michelle. We tried to talk her out of it, but there was no changing her mind."

"What happened after she moved into Patch Lane?"

"Moving into that house was a blessing and a curse. She finally gained the independence that she so desperately sought, but it came at a price. The visions became so intense that the line between reality and vision was slowly fading. She barely slept at night. She always talked about having dreams drawing her to the basement. One day, she finally listened to her dreams and went down into that basement to really look around. She found an old door with a lock on it, which I remember because she even called Samuel over one day to ask him to help her remove the lock. Now you know, we're old fashioned here, so we don't like to get involved in other people's business. Samuel told Michelle not to go snooping and to keep to herself. He refused to help her open that lock. She didn't know how to open it herself without cutting it with bolt cutters, which wasn't an option since she didn't want the landlord to find out."

I thought back to when I first approached Patch Lane and I still saw the rusty lock on the door, so there was no way she could have gotten into that basement room unless she found the underground tunnel. I redirected my thoughts to the landlord. "What do you know about the landlord?"

"Oh, I don't really know who he was. Or she, I suppose. One day Michelle told Samuel that she wrote her rent checks out to *Cash* and Samuel about near had a heart attack. He hollered at Michelle, telling her why she shouldn't go mailing checks addressed to *Cash*, not to mention the fact that she was mailing these checks to a random P.O. Box. Samuel and I always suspected Joseph was still running that farm, but we could never prove it."

I realized that figuring out the owner of Patch Lane was going to be an assignment I would have to pursue on my own. So instead, I followed up and asked, "Then, how did Michelle eventually get into the locked room in the basement?"

"Oddly enough, Michelle wasn't the one who found the root cellar passage, it was Ryan. One day, he was playing in the yard and started jumping around. The loud clank of the metal got Michelle's attention, and she ran over to find Ryan jumping on the root cellar door. She put him inside and went back to investigate. She opened the door, walked down the stairs, and through the tunnel. She came to a hatch, so she opened it. She found herself in that locked room in the basement! She called me right after she found it. I remember it clear as day." A single tear made its way down Rose's cheek, making a path straight over each wrinkle. Rose added, "As soon as Michelle got into that room, she had the worst vision yet. She saw her own death."

The rain turned into a monsoon. Lightning struck in the distance, followed less than two seconds later by rumbling thunder. I took a sip of water and tried to imagine what it would be like to envision my own death. Before I could ask any more questions, Rose continued, "That was really when things got bad. Michelle found things in that room she shouldn't have, and she wanted to go to the police, but for some reason she said she didn't know if she could trust them. Instead, she went straight to the feds. Well, you know where it went from there."

"I actually don't know many of the details since a lot of what happened was documented at the federal level, rather than by Amber Forest PD. So, what exactly did she find in that root cellar?"

"She found an entire assortment of guns. Undocumented guns. She wasn't the kind of girl who was afraid to be in the same room as a gun, so it wasn't so much the guns that startled her, but rather the immense negative energy."

"The energy?"

"Yes. It's hard to explain. You see, Michelle's gift wasn't like that mumbo jumbo you see on TV. She couldn't sit down and tell you the future on demand. She would frequently feel a sense of warmth and happiness with a person, place, or object, or she could also feel heaviness and darkness with the same. It was only on rare occasions that she got true, genuine visions. Even the night that her own sister died, she didn't know *who* had died, but she felt the energy of death close to her. It was always so hard to watch her go through that."

"So, how exactly did she help the police with their cases?"

"Oh, it wasn't like she helped them on a daily basis. It was only on big cases every so often. She could sense people's energies and whether or not they were being truthful with the officers. If they were searching for a body and knew the general area, she would spend days walking around, holding an object of the victim's, and she could be drawn to where their body was. I remember one missing child case she assisted with, she actually saw a vision of the child playing near water, and that the child's foot was stuck, and she couldn't escape. The police ended up finding the missing child down at the river, with her foot stuck under a rock."

I slowly became more open to the notion that Michelle had some form of psychic ability. She sounded like an incredibly interesting and genuinely kind-hearted person. "You said her son, Ryan, was with Michelle's aunt, Regina. Do you stay in contact with them?"

"Oh yes, they call me at least once a week. Ryan recently finished up college down in Maryland and he was considering moving to Pittsburgh for a job with one of those big banks over in the city. He asked me if he could stay here the night before he had an interview. I warned him it's still quite a drive away, but he said he's young and doesn't mind some travel time. I remember a time when a twenty-mile trip was considered an entire day's event. My, how times have changed." Rose's thoughts trailed off and I redirected my original line of questioning.

"Rose, do you know who Ryan's father is?"

Rose nodded her head and answered, "Yes, I do."

I was so engrossed in my conversation with Rose that I was startled when my radio clicked on. I jumped back in my seat at the unexpected sound.

"Dispatch to 1034."

"1034, go ahead."

"Are you 10-4?" Dispatch did a good job checking in with an officer if we had been on scene and they hadn't heard from us for a while.

"Affirmative." I redirected my attention to Rose. "I'm sorry about that."

"Oh no, it's alright. Do you need to get going?"

"No, not at all. They were just making sure I was alright. I was about to ask you who the father of Michelle's child was?"

Rose took a deep breath, "He was a cook at the restaurant Michelle worked at. He forced himself on her one night while they were closing. That job was the only thing she had for quite some time, and she was worried if she said anything, she would end up being the one in trouble. In a town this small, she knew people would talk and gossip. It's a shame how a community can be so close, and yet how quickly it can stab you in the back with gossip."

My heart ached for Michelle. Shortly after my mom died, I was in elementary school and a classmate came up to me and asked me who was going to take care of me now. When I told him that I had my dad to take care of me, he said, "No you don't. I heard my mom and dad talking and they said all your dad does is work and you're at home alone all the time." I was never home alone at that age, not once. My dad made sure to take me to my Aunt Maggie's to watch me or he would adjust his shift hours. My dad made me his entire life, and with every decision he made, he thought of me. I understood exactly what Rose meant by a community so close and yet so quick to gossip. "Oh Rose, I'm so sorry. That must have been so hard for her."

"All we could do was try to help her. She even started trusting men again and started dating someone right around the time she moved to Patch Lane, but she was very secretive about his identity. All she told us was that he was a good man and would be a great father to Ryan, if things went in that direction."

"What did you guys think happened to her twenty years ago?"

"We thought she died in an accident in Pittsburgh. I remember thinking that it was such a miracle she had survived the car accident from when Ryan was born, I figured she must have cheated death."

I began to wonder exactly how the U.S. Marshals pulled off faking Michelle's death. Since Matt wasn't able to provide me many details of the operation, I thought maybe Rose could shed some light. "Did the police find her somewhere? What exactly did they say happened?"

"They really didn't say much. Two young policemen knocked on our front door and told us Michelle was killed in an accident. Ryan was at our house since Michelle had asked us to watch him while she went out to dinner in Pittsburgh with the guy she had been dating. She told us they were going to spend the night in the city, and she would be back the next day. The young officers told us that she had fallen off Mount Washington near the overlook of the city and sustained life-threatening injuries. I was an absolute mess that night, and that year for that matter, but Samuel was so much stronger than me. He had enough strength for us both." Rose began fighting back tears at her memories of Samuel. She wiped her nose with another tissue from her sleeve and continued, "I do remember Samuel asking how such an accident could happen. The Amber Forest officers said that Pittsburgh Police handled the case, so they did not have many details. They were simply requested to notify next of kin."

So that's how they did it. The U.S. Marshals made up some story in the big city, avoiding the small-town gossip, and had Amber Forest PD make notification. No body, no mess, no big hysteria. I began to ask, "So—" but Dispatch interrupted me.

"Dispatch to all units. Please respond to River Road for flash flooding. We received six calls that the river has risen past the road and barricades need to be put up."

"1045, show me en route." Of course, Tim was one of the first to respond. He was one of the most active officers we had.

A few seconds later, the rest of the squad jumped on the radio.

"1039 on my way." Peterson was second in line.

"1052 en route." Redkin was third.

I joined, "1034, you can show me leaving Cranberry Road and I'll be en route." I turned to Rose. "I have so many more questions for you. Would you mind if I stopped back sometime?"

Rose gently threw both of her hands in the air, "Oh of course! You are welcome back here anytime, Sarah. I hope you don't think I'm some crazy old lady."

I assured her that I believed everything she told me and I would love to come by again. She walked me to the door and handed me a hot mug of coffee. "You can bring the mug back the next time you see me."

I thanked Rose and headed down to River Road to start damage control. It took me almost fifteen minutes to get there because of how quickly the roads had flooded. I arrived on scene, immediately ran over to the plywood shed, and began unlocking the old locker-style lock so that we could get the barricades out. I opened the makeshift shed and started handing out barricades to everyone. They had already set up the street cones and blocked off traffic the next street over so we could set up these barricades without incident. This wasn't my first time setting up barricades down at River Road. Heavy rain had definitely caused flooding in the past, so I'd learned to monitor the river on a regular basis. We successfully set up the barricades along the flooded road to prevent any vehicles from falling victim to the rising waters. I ended up spending the rest of the night doing damage control from the flooding.

I was beyond soaking wet, so the first thing I did upon getting home was strip naked, then take a long, hot shower. Hallie's new thing was to sit on the toilet and watch me the entire time. At first, I thought it was creepy, but then I started to think she was concerned I was drowning every time I showered because she always looked so worried as she sat there. I got out of the shower and gave Hallie one of her bedtime treats. *Goddamn, do I love this cat.* I couldn't help but sense that, in some way, my mom had brought her to me.

Chapter 15

Ring. Ring. Ring. Ring.

What the hell? My alarm wouldn't shut off. I soon realized it was my phone. I answered in a groggy voice, "Hello?"

"Hey Sarah, it's Dad. I'm sorry, did I wake you?"

"Yeah, but it's fine. Is everything alright?"

"Oh yeah, yeah, I'm fine. But the basement flooded pretty bad. I was hoping you could stop by here for a few hours before you go back to work tonight to help me move all these boxes upstairs."

Since he'd recently had knee surgery, he couldn't walk up and down the stairs too easily. I never said no to my dad. I'm a daddy's girl, and we've always had each other's backs. "Of course, Dad, I'll be right over. You want me to grab lunch for us? Pizza?"

"You read my mind, sweetie."

I slowly got dressed and allowed myself thirty minutes of sitting on my couch with Hallie catching up on one of my shameful drama shows while I ate a small breakfast. I made sure not to eat too much since I knew I'd need to save room for Tony's Pizza.

I pulled up to my dad's house and carried the pizza in one hand while I opened the front door with my other.

"Dad! Pizza's here!"

He came upstairs and we each scarfed down a couple slices. There's something so complementary about the salty pepperoni and the semi-sweet tomato sauce with just the right amount of greasy cheese that makes Tony's Pizza pure satisfaction.

"You know, Sarah, there was a time when I could have eaten this entire large pizza by myself. My stomach just isn't what it used to be."

I rolled my eyes and laughed as he reminded me for about the twentieth time of his college days. We finished off the box and washed up before heading downstairs to tackle the basement disaster. My dad had already moved several of the boxes by himself.

"Dad, you really should have waited until I got here to do all of this." There was a time when I would have been glad at the thought of having my dad do all the heavy lifting, but ever since a few years ago, around the time that I went through the police academy, I began to worry about him hurting himself, especially considering his recent surgery.

"Don't worry, I still saved a lot for you! Can you help me carry up all these cardboard boxes in this corner? You can set them all in the family room."

I started walking down the basement stairs. As I reached the last step, there was a splash, and I felt my foot become soaked. There was nearly six inches of water in my dad's basement. Amber Forest is an older town, so most of the houses had unfinished basements with nothing more than two rooms and a toilet. There wasn't too much damage down there except for a handful of cardboard boxes that were becoming saturated.

I began carrying boxes upstairs, one by one. My dad had already moved all the boxes from the ground to higher shelves, but he still wanted them upstairs so that they could dry out. Then we could move the stuff out of the cardboard boxes and into the plastic storage bins that he'd bought earlier that morning.

I was taking the last box off his tool bench when I noticed "Theresa" written across the top in big black sharpie. I couldn't help but open it. I was suddenly faced with old photographs, clothing, and drawings of my mom's. I grabbed the stool from under the tool bench and eased myself onto it, still holding a stack of photographs in my other hand. As

I went through them, memories flooded back. My dad joined me, gently taking a few photographs and sharing the moment with me.

He pulled over a step ladder and sat next to me. He quietly admitted, "I miss her so damn much, Sarah. Do you realize how much you look like her?"

I didn't care about being called pretty or gorgeous. Whenever someone told me I looked like my mother, it was the best compliment I could ever receive. I remember praying during my ugly duckling phase in middle school, asking God to make me even half as beautiful as my mother when I grew up. So now, whenever someone tells me I look just like her I can't help but wear a big smile. "I know, Dad, I miss her too. It's hard to believe it's been over twenty years."

We reminisced as we shared old memories, agreeing that it would be smart to go visit my mom's grave later that day, to make sure the flooding hadn't damaged either the cemetery or the flowers that Aunt Maggie regularly kept around her headstone. I pulled down my sleeve and gently wiped my nose as I gathered my composure. I allowed only a few tears to fall, but then got back to work. I continued the cycle of walking up and down the stairs carrying boxes. By about my fourth trip up, one of the boxes was so saturated that the bottom tore open, spilling its contents all over the stairs. I bent down and started picking up old uniform shirts of my dad's and some sports memorabilia that he had tucked away. As I lifted one of the shirts, a photograph fell out and landed on the step below me. I picked it up to see if it was another picture of my mom, and to my surprise, it wasn't. It was a photograph of me from when I was about five years old. I was standing next to some woman at a carnival or fair. *Where do I know her from?* While my brain was processing who the woman in the photograph was, my dad came over and snatched the photograph from my hand.

"What are you doing?!" It wasn't like my dad to yell. I was so confused.

"Dad...I just..." I looked again at the photograph he was now holding in his hand. The wires in my brain finally connected. I knew the identity of the woman in the picture. It was Michelle Kline.

Why is there a photograph of me with Michelle at a fair? It made no sense. I opened my mouth, but nothing came out. I'm not sure if it was shock or utter confusion my dad noticed in me, but as soon as he locked eyes with mine, he knew I'd figured it out.

"How about we go sit down upstairs and talk, Sarah?"

I felt a whirlwind of different emotions rush through my body, and I began to feel dizzy. I grabbed onto the old wooden stair railing and caught my balance. "What the hell is going on, Dad?"

"Sarah, let's just sit down and talk."

As much as I didn't want to go sit down, my body gave me no choice. We went upstairs and I parked myself on the couch. My dad walked into the kitchen and I heard a pop. He came back out with a bottle of merlot in one hand and two glasses in the other. He sat down and poured each of us a glass of wine. "This was always your mother's favorite one," he said with a shaky tone.

I looked up at him and watched as a tear rolled down his cheek, past his mouth, and dripped onto his hand. I needed answers and I needed them now. "Dad, why do you have that photograph?"

He took a long sip of his wine and started to explain. "Oh, where do I even begin? I met Michelle many years ago, only a couple months after your mom passed. I was on duty and got a call for service in the park. Michelle had, um...she'd found something there."

I stopped him. "I spoke with Michelle's grandma, Rose. She told me about Michelle's gift."

My dad's eyebrows raised, and he slowly nodded his head. "Ah, so you know. Well, Michelle sensed that there was a young girl buried in the park and, sure enough, there was. We were all so impressed with her gift, we began using her for help with our unsolved cases. Michelle and I got to spend a lot of time together working those cases, since I was on track to become the Sergeant Detective. We became very good friends. One thing led to another, and we, um, we became romantically involved." My dad glanced down and shook his head. "I was so happy, and yet I felt so guilty and ashamed for being happy so soon after your mother passed. We agreed it would be best not to tell anyone about us. Not only because of your mother, but we knew people would judge our age difference. Whenever we wanted some normalcy, we took you kids to the amusement park in the city and we told you we were friends. That's where that photograph was taken."

"Why didn't you tell me all of this when I started asking you about Patch Lane and about Michelle Kline?" My tone grew louder as I became angry that my dad, who was also my best friend, had lied to me.

"Well, I didn't lie, Sarah. I told you I had been to Patch Lane for that ATF raid, which was true. I had been there before I ever met Michelle. I just left out the fact that I had been there additional times…" He paused, then continued, "And you never actually asked me about Michelle. You only asked me if I had ever been to that house before, then you ran out the door saying you had to go take care of that cat of yours. It wasn't until a few nights ago when you were here talking to Tim about Michelle that I first heard you say her name. My heart stopped when I heard it. I thought she'd died twenty years ago, and that's the God's honest truth. First your mom, then Michelle. I kind of gave up hope after I lost Michelle. Well, at least when I thought I had lost her."

I could feel the anger stir inside my gut. "How the hell can you say that wasn't lying to me?"

"You're right. By omitting the truth, I lied. I'm so sorry, sweetie. I didn't tell you when you were little because of how recently your mom had passed. You barely even understood what death was back then. And as time went on, there was no need to bring up the past."

"So, then, what did happen to Michelle, Dad?"

"Moving into that house was a horrible mistake for her. That house was haunted by its past and its present. Her gift became more of a curse, and I always worried it would be her downfall. She used to see things inside the house. She would see figures run from one room to another. She used to hear the cries of young girls. But then, she saw that she was destined to die in that house. No one should ever have to experience what she did. When she found all the guns in that hidden tunnel and in that room, she called me immediately. She wanted to report it to the police, but I remembered what happened with the ATF raid before she moved into Patch Lane. There was a mole in the department, and they gave Joseph a heads up before the raid so that he would have time to get out of there. He eventually found new hidden root cellars and tunnels and rooms to hide his stuff in all over that farmland. I bet that farm is over a hundred acres. Can you imagine how many hidden root cellars he could have? I gave Michelle the phone number of a friend of mine in ATF and I'm not sure what happened after that, but apparently she ended up in witness protection."

"So, you're saying you had no idea that she was in witness protection all these years?"

"No! I honestly had no idea." My dad began choking up, which was unlike him. The only time I had ever seen my dad become emotional was when we talked about my mom, or when he mentioned our old dog that he had to have put down due to bone cancer. I began to feel sorry for my dad. I could tell that he was grieving Michelle's death, her real death, but I couldn't get past my anger at him for not telling me all these things. I was losing trust in the one person I trusted most in this world and it caused me to start second guessing everyone else I believed in.

"Were you in Pittsburgh with her the night of her alleged accident?"

"No, I wasn't. I heard the rumor that she went to Pittsburgh for a date and at first, I was in denial that she could cheat on me, but then as time went on, I fell victim to the lie and was so angry with her. Oh, all of these years I was so hurt by her, but now I can see that she never cheated on me, it was all to save her life." My dad caught a sob in his throat and swallowed it back down.

How could I trust anything that my dad was saying after learning he lied all these years? He was my best friend and we were supposed to have each other's backs. "And Tim?! Did he know all of this and lie to me, too?" I was screaming by that point.

"What? Tim? Oh God no, he didn't know anything. He's a straight arrow, Sarah, you know that. He's there when you need him, follows the rules, and never sticks his nose where it shouldn't be. He still doesn't know any of this. He was only a rookie around the time Michelle was at Patch Lane. He certainly had no idea she was helping with our cases, and Chief Clark wanted to keep it hush."

I could feel the smoke pouring from my ears. I chugged the rest of my wine and stormed out the door. My dad called out for me to wait, but I kept going. The hurt and pain I felt went beyond emotion, it became physical. My stomach hurt, my face felt hot as hell, and everything was spinning. How could he betray me like that and lie to me after all these years? I sped home, rushed through my front door, and, before even undressing, opened a new bottle of Riesling. I opted for a white this time because I was in the mood for chugging, not sipping. I didn't know how to cope with stress, but I knew how to drink.

I struggled with wrapping my head around the fact that I knew Michelle Kline. I quickly emailed Sergeant Oakley and told him I was going to use an unscheduled vacation day because of some personal family matters. Sergeant Oakley may be tough, but he was a firm believer that if you weren't one hundred percent mentally at work, then you needed to take a vacation day, because you were only putting your life and your coworkers' lives at risk by being there.

I grabbed my glass of Riesling and headed to my bathroom. I ran the bath water, added some bubble bath, and tested the water with my right toes first. *Ah, perfect.* I stripped down and slid into the tub, closing my eyes as I slid under the water. I could hear the rain outside my bathroom window beating down rhythmically. It hadn't stopped raining since my visit to Rose's. While I hated the flooding and the horror that came with the rain, I enjoyed listening to the sound of it on my window.

I grabbed my drawing journal and started to drunkenly sketch the first things that came to my mind. I had so much built up emotion from my visit with my dad that I had to release my energy, and drinking wasn't going to be enough. I pressed my graphite hard against the paper, slowly releasing to a lighter pressure. I don't know how long I sat there engrossed in the process, but when I was finished, I set the journal down on my coffee table and took another drink of wine. I stared at the drawing of the rose bush and felt a whole new wave of emotion wash over me. This wasn't anger or betrayal. This was grief. All at once, I was hit with the grief of missing my mom. I thought I was angry that my dad had lied, but I was actually angry that he had fallen in love with a woman who wasn't Mom. Hallie instinctually came over and curled up on my lap. I cried so hard that my entire sleeve was drenched in tears, which forced me to get up and grab a box of tissues. I couldn't even remember the last time I had truly grieved over the loss of my mom. I cried so hard that, between the wine and the tears, I felt dehydrated and eventually passed out on my couch.

Chapter 17

"Is everything okay?"

It was thoughtful of Matt to call me when I didn't show up for work. "Yeah, I just needed a mental health day because of a conversation I had with my dad. How did you know I wasn't at work tonight?"

"I stopped by because I had some information I wanted to fill you in on relating to Joseph's whereabouts. Will you be back at work tomorrow?"

"Yeah, I'll be back in tomorrow. You want me to ask Oakley if I can come in early?"

"That would be great. Actually, I'm at the station now so I'll talk to Oakley for ya. See ya tomorrow."

"Thanks! Bye."

I went into the station early Sunday morning, as promised. Matt wasn't there yet, so I used the opportunity to run down the street and grab a nice, strong cup of coffee, and ordered an extra one to give to Matt since it seemed like he was having a slow-moving day. By the time I got back to the station, Matt had already arrived, so I handed him his cup of coffee.

"Oh awesome, thanks." He took a sip. "Ah Jesus, no cream or sugar?"

"Sorry, I wasn't sure how you liked it. We have cream and sugar in the break room, though, if you want to go add some."

"Who in their right mind doesn't use at least one or the other?"

"I drink my coffee black. That's the best way to really savor the flavor of the beans." I took a sip from my cup and dramatically added, "Mmm…real flavor. Not just milk and sugar."

We both laughed, and I showed Matt to the cream and sugar in the break room. Betty Ann was sitting in there talking on her phone. She suddenly hushed her conversation when we came in, and quickly walked out. That woman could be friendly and energetic one minute, then brash and short the next. Tim once told me that he had a better chance at predicting the lottery than Betty Ann's mood.

"Well, since we have the break room to ourselves, why don't we sit down for a minute and I can tell you about what I have on Joseph Muller."

We both sat down and Matt pulled out some folders and papers from his briefcase.

"Alright. So, I was able to pull Joseph's information up in CLEAN and found out that this guy is older than I realized. He's in his late sixties now, and I was able to pull up his old driver's license photograph that was taken in 1995."

CLEAN is the database for Pennsylvania law enforcement officers to access driver's license and motor vehicle information. Matt took out a photograph from one of the folders and slid it across the table to me.

He continued, "That's Joseph. Well, that was Joseph over twenty years ago. I can only imagine that his blonde hair has either turned grey or fallen out by now. Same goes for his beard. For the most part, he's been completely untraceable since 1997, after the ATF raid. After we found that other root cellar three days ago, ATF brought out their fancy equipment and have been finding underground rooms and tunnels all over that farm. You wouldn't believe the shit they found. There is an entire underground tunnel system connecting over a dozen different rooms. Joseph made those tunnels hidden so that if one of the underground rooms was found, it wouldn't mean the tunnels and other rooms would necessarily be found. The guns in the storage shed back in 1997 were only the tip of the iceberg."

I studied the photograph and all of the information Matt had set in front of me. "What's your plan to find Joseph if he's untraceable?"

Matt smiled with excitement. "We know he hasn't left the area because of all the guns we found all over his property. So, then, the next question is where is he living? It looks like he only used Patch Lane for the guns. He knows he's been found so he might be on the run or could be planning an escape. We're getting really damn close, Sarah. We're going to run 24/7 surveillance on the farm and hope that he's actually stupid enough to return. One thing is for sure, though—Joseph's spooked."

Chapter 18

THUD. Hallie and I suddenly woke from a deep sleep. At first, I thought I imagined the loud noise, but when I realized that Hallie was just as startled, I knew it must have been real. As I went to get out of bed, tires screeched outside my bedroom window as a car raced off. I grabbed my robe and my Glock off my nightstand and ran to the front door. Lying on the front porch was the head of a pig with a note tied around its ear. I shut the door and ran back inside to get some latex gloves from my duty bag. I returned to the front porch and bent over to read the note.

Keep digging and this won't be the only dead pig.

I left the pig's head and the note on my front porch, since I knew if I brought it inside, I would risk Hallie making my evidence her breakfast. I called Matt, and it was only fifteen minutes before he was at my apartment.

Matt asked me if I saw who left the pig's head or if I saw the vehicle, and I felt ashamed to admit that I saw absolutely nothing. I felt like a terrible witness.

"We know Joseph was in business with some dangerous people. It's exactly why we put Michelle into WITSEC. I'm thinking this looks like a mafia message."

I remembered hearing from several people about Joseph's involvement with the mafia, but I struggled to imagine who or where this alleged mafia was. I always thought of the mafia as old Italian guys in New York City or Boston. I asked, "Where the hell are there mafia members anymore? They don't even offer mafia trainings at the police academy. All of the specialized trainings related to organized crime are for street gangs or motorcycle gangs."

"Yeah, I know the mafia isn't exactly what it used to be, but that doesn't mean it doesn't exist anymore. We still have a substantial amount of mafia involvement in Pittsburgh. I wouldn't be surprised if it's the Pittsburgh members who get their guns from Amber Forest, or they could have members who live here to do their grunt work along with Joseph. Sure, Pittsburgh has some farms and land, but it's nowhere near the amount of remoteness and privacy that Amber Forest offers."

"Do I need to worry about this?" I tried my best not to sound afraid, but I was. I felt so vulnerable.

"No. I'm going to make sure someone has eyes on your place throughout this investigation. The FBI has a very strong case they're working against the mafia activity in this area. I can't tell you the details of their investigation because, honestly, I don't even know the details. They know that Joseph Muller is a primary suspect in a homicide case and believe he was involved in mafia activity. They confirmed that Muller did business with the mafia, but said according to their findings and informants, Muller was not actually *in* the mafia. When I asked if they wanted to interview Muller, they said they didn't need him for the case they're building. The FBI is technically in charge of our murder case, but they delegated the legwork to the Marshals, AKA me. Once the mafia sees that you only want to arrest Muller and not pursue them, they should back off."

I took a deep breath and sighed in slight relief. I still questioned, "But how will they know that I'm not trying to pursue them?"

Matt laughed, "Well for starters, you won't be investigating or questioning them after you arrest Muller. Secondly, it's the mafia. They have eyes and ears everywhere. There have been strong suspicions for a while that they even have a mole in one of the law enforcement agencies in the area."

I wasn't sure if Matt's second comment made me feel any more at ease, or just more anxious. "But why are they sending *me* a message? Why aren't they threatening the ATF or you?"

"I can't speak for the mafia, but if I had to guess I would say it's because their M.O. is to control the local police. I'm sure they have an influence on at least one officer in your department already, if not more. They interpret your perseverance as threatening. You have done a lot of investigating with this case well above and beyond what a normal patrol cop would do. They're honestly probably afraid of you and think you're going to target them next. They know they can't influence the ATF, so they won't even try."

I suddenly became aware that I was wearing stained sweatpants and a tank top, since I didn't have a chance to put real clothes on. I excused myself to go shower while Matt and some other officers took notes and photographs and bagged the pig and the note. Technically, the pig's head was evidence and needed to be processed. All I could think was that I did not want to be the one to tell the lab technician they would need to process a dead pig.

I took a long, hot shower, and closed my eyes as I let the steam fill my lungs. Hallie sat on the toilet and watched me the entire time, as she normally does. I spent the majority of the time just letting the hot water roll down my body, barely taking much time to actually lather with soap. I finally got out of the shower, wrapped my towel around me, and wrung my hair out over the sink. *Shit.* I wasn't used to having other people in my apartment when I showered, so I didn't think to bring my clothes into the bathroom with me. I had left my dirty clothes in the sink, which were now wet. I certainly didn't want to put on soggy, dirty clothes. After weighing the options, I decided to make a dash for my bedroom.

I opened the bathroom door and let Hallie go first. I began my hurried pace through the family room and towards my bedroom when I saw Matt standing in the middle of the family room. *Damnit.*

He chuckled at the sight of my half-naked, hurried walk. "Hey, Sarah, sorry to bother you, but everyone was done here, and I didn't want us all to leave without saying anything to you. I'm going to head out to my car and hang outside your place for a few hours until Chief Fox can find a patrol officer to come park out front."

I felt like a goddamn child who needed a babysitter. "No, I'll be fine, you really don't have to stay."

"Well, when the mafia comes knocking on your door, I think it's best to not be alone for a few days."

I couldn't argue with his logic. Matt walked out to his car, and I continued drying off and got dressed. Once I was decent, I went outside and offered to let him come in and hang out in my family room with the television, rather than sit in his car alone for hours. I started to prepare a pot of coffee and he stopped me. "Whoa, are you putting chocolate chips in the coffee?"

"Yeah, I add them to the coffee grounds because it adds a slight mocha flavor to the coffee as it brews. Don't worry, I have milk and sugar you can still add in after it's done."

Matt looked like he'd just solved world hunger. "Holy shit. That's genius."

I laughed and responded, "I guess I never really thought much of it. It's how my dad always makes his coffee. He adds a few chocolate chips and a sprinkle of cinnamon." *Ugh, my dad.* I hadn't talked to him since our argument and I was really missing him. I was still upset and hurt that he'd lied to me, but he was my best friend. I needed to give him the chance to make things right again.

I mostly trusted Matt by now, but I still didn't divulge every piece of information about Patch Lane. I didn't tell him about the shady figure I saw run down into the basement and I didn't tell him about Rose yet. But I thought it would be alright to tell Matt about the receipt that I had found in Michelle's pocket. I explained to him that I found it in her pocket and sent it to the lab for processing.

"So, what was written on the receipt?" Matt asked.

I realized I still hadn't heard back from the Pennsylvania State Police Forensic Lab. "I actually don't know. The lab never got back to me. I was going to call them today. I just thought you should know."

I dialed the phone number I had saved in my phone for the forensic lab.

A woman answered, "Hello, Pennsylvania State Police Forensic Department."

"Hello, this is Officer Hastings following up on the Patch Lane case. I wanted to check the status of my evidence."

"Please hold for a moment while I check that out for you." The receptionist sounded very friendly and only kept me on hold for a minute before she got back on the phone. "Hi, Officer Hastings?"

"Yes, I'm still here."

"It looks like they finished up processing your evidence today. I'm going to transfer you to the technician who completed the analysis so he can explain it to you."

"Alright, thank you. I appreciate it."

I heard a few beeps and another two rings. This time a man answered. "James Decker."

"Hi, Mr. Decker, this is Officer Hastings with the Amber Forest Police Department. I was told that you completed processing my evidence from my case and I wanted to ask what you found written on the back of the receipt. Were you able to make it out?"

"Oh, yeah. Hey there!" I could hear James chewing on something crunchy between his words. "Yeah, that was an interesting one. Let me find my... Oh, here it is! Okay, it said, are you ready?"

I grabbed my pen and a notepad. "Yeah, I'm ready. Go."

"It said: R36 – L12 – R48."

I wrote down the message. "What the hell does that mean?" I asked rhetorically.

To my surprise, James responded, "Well, I can't say for certain, but that definitely looks like a lock combination to me."

"Well?" Matt asked me as I hung up the phone. "What did he say?"

"It's a goddamn lock combination."

Chapter 18

My new babysitter sat in his cruiser outside my bedroom window. I peeked through my blinds and could just make out enough of the shiny head to tell that it was Peterson. I offered him some coffee, even though I already knew what his answer would be. He was grateful for the offer and commented on how good it was. I hung outside with him for a few minutes and told him to feel free to come inside if he needed to use the bathroom or anything else.

Given the circumstances, Sergeant Oakley made the executive decision to give me free reign to adjust my hours as needed. I think he just got annoyed with me calling every other day asking to come in early to do follow up work. Matt planned on asking his ATF connections if they had run into a safe or a locked box of any sort during their most recent search at Patch Lane. I was waiting for the phone call to hear what our next step was going to be, but to my surprise, it was almost noon and I still hadn't heard from Matt.

There was a knock at my door. *Jesus, Peterson. You already have to pee again?* I went over to let Peterson in to use my bathroom for the third time, but was surprised to see Tim standing there.

"Tim? What are you doing here?" Tim always had Tuesdays and Wednesdays off from work like me.

"Well, they posted the job of your babysitter on the overtime board so I figured I could make a few easy extra bucks. Are you working today? I can't keep track with your schedule anymore."

"That is an excellent question. I thought I was going to do some follow up work with the suit, but I haven't heard from him yet. Looks like I'm actually able to relax today. Any chance you'd want to go back to Patch Lane with me tomorrow to check something out? I'm sure Oakley would approve a few hours of overtime for it."

Tim gave me a blank stare. "Hastings. The last time I did that shit with you I had paperwork for days explaining how we found that root cellar and the underground tunnel. Not to mention all the interviews with the suits I had to go through. You really think it's a good idea to go back there without the feds?"

Tim had a good point. I was being impatient as I waited for Matt to call me with an update, so I had a new suggestion for Tim. "Alright, I hear you. What if I called Deputy Sloan up and asked him if he would be alright with us checking out Patch Lane tomorrow, then?"

Tim squinted his eyes as he mulled the thought over. "Yeah. I guess." Tim reached down for his cigarettes. "Do you mind if I have a smoke on your front porch?"

"Not at all, I'll keep you company out here if you'd like."

"Great. I actually wanted to talk to you about your dad."

My dad. Just thinking about him sent a wave of anger over my body and created a pit in my stomach.

Tim added, "He's, uh, he's really upset, Sarah. I don't want to get involved with anything, but I have to be honest, I've never seen him so upset. He wouldn't tell me what happened between you two, but he said you're mad at him."

It only took a matter of seconds before that wave of anger slipped into a wave of grief. I was being selfish by staying mad at my dad while he was mourning the death of Michelle, someone he truly loved. How could I have only thought of myself and not empathized with him, realizing how much he needed me there for him? I was the only person who even knew about him and Michelle, so I was the only one he could talk to. It's sad how easily anger can consume and conquer empathy.

"Thanks, Tim. Maybe I'll try to go see him today."

Tim nodded as he finished his cigarette.

We went back inside, and I called Matt to let him know I wanted to go back to Patch Lane the next day. The phone rang about six times, and right as I thought the voicemail was going to pick up, Matt answered.

"Hey, Sarah. I wasn't able to get a hold of my ATF contact yesterday, but I spoke with him today. He's going to ask around the rest of his team to see if anyone came across a safe or a lock of any kind and hasn't gotten back to me yet."

"Oh, that's alright. I was actually calling to make sure it would be alright if I went back to Patch Lane tomorrow with Tim. Are your guys and ATF done processing the scene?"

"Yeah, they're done. If you want to go back and look for a safe, you'll need a new search warrant. I can apply for one based on the safe combination you found on the receipt in our victim's pocket, since we didn't have that piece of information at the time we applied for the first search warrant." Matt sounded eager to help, but he also sounded exhausted.

"Yeah, that would be great. You sound pretty tired. Are you going to take today off and relax for once?"

"Jesus, you sound like my mother. Yeah, I'm laying low today and going to do a little bit more digging on my laptop. Meet tomorrow morning at the station?"

"Works for me. See you then." I hung up the phone and told Tim that Matt was going to handle the search warrant and join us the next day.

I decided now was as good a time as any to go see my dad. I got dressed and was about to leave when I realized that Tim was still sitting on my couch.

"Hey Tim, question. So, are you supposed to like be my bodyguard or are you supposed to just sit on my house?"

Tim seemed confused by the question, but when he saw my purse in one hand, he realized I was leaving. "Oh, uh, actually, nobody specified. You want me to go somewhere with you?"

"Oh no, I'm only going over to my dad's. I have my Glock with me, and you know my dad has his entire armory to protect me. Just hang out here and get the free money."

Tim shrugged and began to head back to his cruiser. He stopped and turned around to add, "I'm glad you're going to go see your dad. He's a good guy, you know."

I smiled and corrected Tim, "The best."

Chapter 19

I knocked on my dad's front door using the side of my shoe. I would have let myself in, but I was too busy balancing an apology pepperoni pizza in one hand and a six pack of my dad's favorite IPA in the other. I wasn't sure if it was the pizza, beer, or me, but a huge smile came across his face when he opened the door.

"Sarah! I'm happy you came back. I wanted to sort things out with you. I hate how we left things on Saturday."

I guess it was me that caused the huge smile after all. "Yeah Dad, I'm really sorry, too. I brought your favorite combination—pizza and beer." I raised up the six pack, as if he couldn't already see it.

We sat down and filled our stomachs with as much food and drink as we could handle. When we were satisfied we had eaten enough pizza and were only working on our beers, I broke the silence.

"Dad, I'm sorry I overreacted before. I was so busy thinking about how upset I was that you didn't tell me about Michelle that I didn't even think to consider how hard this must be for you to cope with. Learning about her death for a second time must be devastating. I think I also might have overreacted to the idea of you being with another woman besides Mom and that was selfish of me."

My dad took a long chug of his beer. "Yeah. It's been really hard to accept that she lied to me all of these years that she was in hiding. But you know what, it also made me realize how hurt you must have felt that I kept this hidden from you." He let out a sad chuckle. "I guess we both did a lot of thinking these past couple days, huh?"

Yeah, a lot of thinking and a lot of drinking. I kept my thoughts to myself.

"So, any leads as to who killed her?" my dad asked.

"We're homing in on Muller. He had every motive to want Michelle dead, and we know that he's been at Patch Lane this whole time in and out of old root cellars and tunnels throughout the property."

"Yeah, that makes sense." My dad shook his head slightly and added, "But that still doesn't explain why she came out of hiding after twenty years."

"We still haven't figured that out either. However, I talked to the PA state lab today and I got an interesting result on what she had written on the back of an old receipt that was in her pocket."

My dad's curiosity was piqued. He tightened his forehead and leaned in closer. "What was on it?"

"A combination to some type of lock, or possibly a safe."

"Hmm…" My dad's eyes moved from one side of the room to the other as he fell into deep thought. "You know what, I remember her saying something about a safe."

I jolted straight up and exclaimed, "Wait, what? What do you know about a safe of hers?"

My dad held both of his hands up in defense. "Whoa now, I don't have all the answers here so don't get your hopes up. I just remember she had asked me about safes and where to get one. She knew I had several in the house to keep my guns locked up to prevent you from accidentally finding one. I told her I got my safe from Dudley's gun store down the road and she said she was going to check it out. She probably asked me about that a week or so before she died. Or, uh, went into the Witness Protection Program, I guess." He was visibly upset, remembering the lie he was fed.

"Do you have any idea where she would have put the safe?"

The lines on my dad's forehead lifted and his eyes opened further. "I honestly have no idea." He glanced away as a thought trailed through his mind. "Actually...in that same conversation she was asking me about where she could find cheap hardwood planks, because she said Ryan was jumping around and cracked her floor. It's a far stretch, but I wonder if she wanted to hide the safe below her floor or something."

I leaned over and gave my dad a big kiss on the cheek. "Dad, you have been more than helpful! How about we finish this six pack off and watch our movie?"

Before my dad could even say yes, he was out of his seat and hunched over in front of the television stand. "*Blazing Saddles* it is!"

Patch Lane

Chapter 20

I got to the station and found Tim and Matt were already waiting for me.

"Hey Sarah, you ready to go?" Matt grabbed his keys from his pocket.

"Yeah, I'm all set."

I wanted to let Matt and Tim in on the information I'd received from my dad, but there was no way to tell them without explaining the entire situation, which I was not prepared to do. Tim and I loaded ourselves into Matt's Forester and we headed down to Patch Lane.

We turned down the gravel lane and Matt asked, "Alright, so anyone have a plan?"

Tim responded, "Well don't look at me. I'm only here because Hastings bribed me with the OT pay."

I rolled my eyes. "Yeah, well, don't act like I had to twist your arm too much. I'm thinking we can search the house top to bottom and look for anywhere that a safe or something similar could be hidden. Whatever Michelle came back to this house to open, she had to have hidden it somewhere that she knew it would never be found."

Tim and I let Matt cut the tape across the front door. We all agreed to start at the top and work our way down. We walked upstairs and first searched the room immediately to the right of the landing. There was no furniture left in the house so there wasn't much digging we could do. Tim checked the closet while Matt closely examined the walls. I thought back to what my dad had told me, and I slowly got down onto my knees and began checking the floorboards.

Tim looked at me with confusion. "What the hell are you doing?"

"I'm checking to see if any floorboards are loose."

"Oh. Yeah, I guess that's a good idea." Tim got down onto his knees and began helping me check the floorboards.

We finished searching the entire bedroom with absolutely no leads. We made our way down the short hallway and into the second bedroom. Matt continued closely checking the walls while Tim and I examined all the floorboards. I started on the left half of the room and worked my way down the walls, circling towards the center of the room, while Tim mirrored my movements on the other side. I pushed down on each end of the floorboards, waiting to see if any popped up. We had no luck.

The only thing left untouched in the bedroom was the closet. Rather than having the door perfectly flush with the ground, it was about a foot higher, so you would have to step up and into the closet. I thought this was a weird way for a closet to be set up until I remembered from the first time I searched the house that the closet doubled as the first step towards the attic. I opened the door, and there was a second door at the back of the closet with a stairwell that led to an attic. I took my flashlight off my duty belt and said, "Hey guys, there's an attic up here. Come on."

We headed up into the attic, keeping the same routine as before. Matt checked the walls while Tim and I went over the floor. *Damnit.* Still no luck. I really thought we were going to find something up there. We headed back downstairs, and as Tim was about to step off the closet ledge and back into the bedroom, a loose floorboard shot up under his weight, causing him to trip over it and fall forward. The single plank completely dislodged from the floor, clattering to the floor alongside Tim.

"What the hell?!" Tim rolled over, and we all examined the area where he stumbled. Matt and I cautiously walked around the hole in the floor and I grabbed hold of the adjacent floorboards, easily lifting each one up and out of the closet until I could see the safe sitting below.

It was a small, black safe. I reached down and brought it up from below the floor. Matt, Tim, and I all looked at each other. I reached into my front vest pocket and took out my notepad. It read, "R36 – L12 – R48."

I spun the lock three times to the right to clear it. The fourth time I spun the lock until it stopped on 36. I spun the lock two times to the left, stopping on 12. Finally, I spun the lock once to the right, and stopped at 48. *Click.* The safe unlatched.

I opened the safe while Matt and Tim locked their eyes onto it. There was a document with an official seal resting on top of other items. I took it out and saw it was a Pennsylvania birth certificate for Ryan Kline. Underneath, there were several photographs. I took the small stack from the safe and noticed the top photograph was of Michelle and a young boy, who I presumed to be Ryan. I flipped through a few more photographs of Michelle and various family members, including Rose. My heart stopped when I came across a photograph of Michelle, Ryan, my dad, and me.

I couldn't control the wave of emotion I felt crash into me. I started crying as the realization hit me that not only my dad, but also I, meant so much to Michelle that she locked a photograph of us away in her safe.

Matt asked, "Sarah, what's wrong?"

Tim took the photograph from my hands. "Holy shit."

Oh God, he knows. I was able to momentarily stop my tears and sniffed my nose. "Tim, please."

Tim was in shock. "Sarah."

I knew I was in trouble when he used my first name.

He continued, "Why the hell is there a picture of you and your dad with Michelle and her son? What aren't you telling us?"

Matt had no idea what my dad looked like, and certainly didn't know what I looked like when I was a child. He asked, "Wait. Is that really you and your dad in that picture? That doesn't make any sense." He took a step backwards. "Sarah…"

In a shaky voice, I answered them both, "Guys, I'm sorry. I didn't tell you because it wasn't my position to, it's my dad's business. He used to date Michelle right before she went into WITSEC. He really loved her. He never told me until a few days ago when I found a picture of her at his house. He had no idea she ever went into WITSEC and he's been coping with accepting her real death while I've been coping with accepting their relationship."

Tim leaned his back against the wall in disbelief. "I can't believe I had no idea." He leaned over, resting his hands on his knees. "Alright, we have to think this through. So, your dad knew Michelle and he was serious with her. Which means you knew her, whether or not you actually remember her. Sarah, you need to tell Chief about this, or at least tell Oakley. This is a major conflict of interest."

"There's no conflict of interest," I spat back at him. "I'm fine handling this case. I didn't even know her, and we all know my dad isn't involved with her murder." *I'm fine.* That seemed to be my new life motto.

Matt intervened, "Well that might all be true, but I would highly suggest being honest with your chain of command and explaining the situation to them. You don't want to ruin your career by not providing full disclosure to your superiors. I'm going to have to tell my superiors about this, too."

I thought about what Matt had said but didn't respond.

Tim stood up. "I hate to do this, but you know I can't lie for you. Either you tell Oakley, or I will."

I couldn't believe Tim was forcing my hand in this situation. I knew he was a straight arrow, but it was really annoying. I finally agreed. "Fine. Let's just go."

Chapter 21

I went in to work Thursday night, this time for my regular shift. I had worked odd days and hours the past week and this was the first time in a while I was present at roll call. After Sergeant Oakley dismissed us, I asked if we could talk. I followed him to his office and shut the door behind me.

"Geez, Hastings, must be important for you to shut the door. What's going on?"

I took a seat. "Sarge, there's something I need to tell you about the Patch Lane case, but it's incredibly private and I ask that you keep this information to yourself."

"Alright. Go ahead."

I rubbed my hand against my forehead. My mouth went dry and my sentences were dotted with too many *ums* and stutters as I briefly explained how my father and I knew the victim. Before Sergeant Oakley could respond to my bomb of information, I quickly added, "I was so young, though, I swear I don't remember ever meeting her."

Sergeant Oakley's eyebrows raised up and he quietly muttered, "What the...?"

I jumped back into what I was saying. "I know this might appear like a conflict of interest, which is why I wanted to disclose this to you right away. I only found everything out this week."

"How long have you known?"

"Not long."

"Tell me exactly how long you've known that you used to know Kline?"

"I found out last Saturday. Five days."

Sergeant Oakley's face grew red and his brows scrunched up. It was apparent he was pissed as he spoke with heated words, "You've known for five goddamn days and are just telling me this now? Hastings, you know I always have your back, but it's not okay under any circumstance to lie to me. And you know damn well that omitting the truth is lying in my book."

"I'm sorry, Sarge."

"I know you want to keep this under wraps, but you know I'm going to have to run this by Chief to sign off on. It's up to him to decide whether this is a conflict of interest and whether or not you can stay on the case."

It was no secret that Chief Fox was not fond of me. He would take me off the case the first chance he got. "Sarge, please, you know Fox has it out for me. We're getting close, I just need a little bit more time to prove that I can close this case. Nobody is better for it than I am."

Sergeant Oakley sat back in his chair. "I know, I know. But I can't have my ass on the line here. Here's what I can do. Whenever I talk to Chief tomorrow, I can strongly suggest that he lets me keep you on this case. But you know I sure as hell can't control what he decides to do."

"Yeah, I understand. Thanks."

Sergeant Oakley added, "Oh by the way, before you hit the road tonight, can you check to see if we ever got the lab results back from that fatal car accident a couple weeks ago? I meant to ask someone during roll call to check and it slipped my mind. The lab left me a voicemail saying they faxed them over this evening. I'm thinking they must have sent it after Betty Ann had already left for the day."

"Yeah, no problem." I left Sergeant Oakley's office and headed towards Betty Ann's desk.

I checked the fax machine but found nothing. There was a stack of paper sitting under Betty Ann's desk, on top of a two-drawer filing cabinet. It was the only paper sitting out. I thought maybe she could have gotten the fax right before she left and set it aside to take care of in the morning. I grabbed the pages and began to go through them. They were mostly time sheet records and a few letters addressed to the chief. As I was glancing through each one individually, I stopped when I saw my name. There was a letter written to me.

Dear Officer Hastings,

My name is Ryan Kline. I was told that you are currently investigating my mother's death. I think I might have some information that could help you with your investigation. Please give me a call at your earliest convenience.

Ryan Kline

At the bottom of the letter was a phone number. I had no idea when he'd sent it, so I looked for the corresponding envelope to see if there was a date stamped on it. I had no luck finding it. I folded up the letter and put it in my cargo side pocket. Betty Ann did not appear to be the most organized secretary, and I was beginning to see why Sergeant Oakley had asked me to double check for the lab results. I finished reviewing the stack of papers, and towards the bottom I found the lab results he'd requested. I grabbed them off the stack and took them back to Sergeant Oakley's office.

I would have to wait until morning to call Ryan, since it was the middle of the night and he probably wouldn't appreciate a phone call at this hour.

Patch Lane

Chapter 22

Anxiety flooded my veins as I drove to the station. I knew that when Sergeant Oakley called me and said Chief Fox wanted to see me as soon as possible, it was not a good sign. I hadn't even gotten a chance to call Ryan yet. When I'd woken up, I'd already had a voicemail from Sergeant Oakley.

My heart raced faster as I walked up the stairs towards Chief Fox's office. I tried to read his expression when I walked in, but I couldn't tell if he was angry or just extremely focused on what he was reading on his computer.

"Hastings, take a seat." He sounded more annoyed than angry.

I sat down.

"Sergeant Oakley stayed late past shift this morning so that he could talk to me when I got into the office. He told me about your conflict with the Patch Lane case."

"There's no conflict, Chief." I knew that interrupting him was a mistake, but the words flew out of my mouth before I could stop them.

Chief Fox sat straight up and tilted his head slightly. "I wasn't finished talking yet. As I was saying, I found out about your conflict with the Patch Lane case. The fact that both you and your dad knew our victim makes you too close to this thing. You're not in any trouble, but you can thank Oakley for that. I was ready to suspend you for not telling us this information sooner. You're back on patrol, and no more following up on the Patch Lane case or on anything that relates to Michelle Kline. You got it?"

"There's no reason to take me off this case. I've spent three weeks on this, and we are getting so close to finding Joseph Muller. Chief, you know I'm the best officer for this case. I don't even remember ever meeting Michelle Kline. This isn't right."

What was once annoyance turned to anger. "Who the hell do you think you are, sweetheart? I'm the chief. This isn't a negotiation. I'm telling you that you're off this case. I can't have the Amber Forest Police Department get backlash for letting one of its officers investigate the murder of her father's mistress. Forget it."

I jumped out of my chair and stormed out of his office. I stopped myself from slamming his door behind me, which probably would have at a minimum gotten me written up. *How could I be off the case?* My blood was boiling.

I got home and found Hallie waiting for me on the couch. Somehow, all it took was the sight of her to calm me down. I laid down on the couch and gave Hallie all the snuggles she would tolerate. I was desperate for wine, but I wasn't sure if I was going to be expected to go in to work later since I had already been called in during the day. I wasn't in the mood to talk to anyone, so I sent a brief text to Sergeant Oakley and asked if I had to come in to work that night. He responded and said that, due to how my day went, he recommended that I take a night off to cool down. As soon as I read the last word of the text, I was up and off the couch and headed towards the kitchen for a bottle of wine. I stopped myself right as I was about to open a new bottle, realizing that I was physically shaking from my anxiety. I have a tendency to keep my emotions so bottled up that they manifest physically.

The more I thought about being kicked off the case and the way Chief Fox had treated me, the more my hands shook. I set the bottle of wine back on the counter and changed into my running gear instead. It was time to head outside for a long, hard run. I started out fast, feeling my feet slam against the asphalt as my breaths grew more rapid. The angrier I got, the faster I ran. The air that initially felt cool against my face suddenly felt like ice. I reached up to touch my cheeks and realized they were soaked. I slowed my pace and let the tears flood. I gathered my composure and ran back to my apartment, this time at a steady pace. It felt good to release not only emotionally, but physically. My body needed this.

As soon as I opened my door, my phone alerted me that I'd received another text message. *Ugh, what else does Sarge have to say?* I picked up my phone off the coffee table, still huffing, and looked at the screen. It was from Matt.

Hey, how did today go?

I really wasn't in the mood to talk to anyone about Chief pulling me off the case, but I also knew that this was probably pretty important to tell Matt so that I didn't hold up his investigation. I told him what happened, and, to my surprise, he told me to stay put because he was on his way to my place.

I hurriedly showered, and right as I put some clothes on, there was a knock at my door. I let Matt in, and before I could even offer him a drink or a place to sit, Hallie was wrapping herself around the leg of his black suit.

"Oh, I'm sorry about her, she's getting hair all over you." I attempted to shoo Hallie away from Matt, but he stopped me.

"Don't worry about it. I'm an animal lover." He bent down and gave Hallie a few scratches that she was desperately begging to receive.

I offered Matt a glass of water as I cleared the blankets off the couch to give him room to sit.

Matt sat down and stared at me. His tone suddenly became serious and he said, "I wanted to check in on you."

I was surprised at his concern. "I'm fine. Chief Fox is an idiot and hates me." *There I go again, "I'm fine."*

Matt inhaled and held his breath for a moment. He finally released and I could tell he was preparing to tell me something that he knew I would not want to hear. "Sarah…can you really blame Chief Fox for taking you off of this case?"

Was Matt turning against me now? "Uh, yeah. Of course, I do."

"Alright. Think about it this way. If you're investigating a woman's murder, who are some of the first suspects?"

Where was he going with this? "Well I need more details than that. But I guess I would say whoever saw her last, her husband, or any boyfriends."

Matt nodded as I spoke. "Right, right. Okay. Now given all our facts about Michelle Kline, we know she did not have a husband. Now who was her boyfriend?"

I thought for a moment. *Oh my God. My dad.* "Are you trying to tell me that my dad is your primary suspect?" My words grew louder with anger.

"I'm not saying that he is automatically a suspect, but he is definitely someone who needs to be verified and checked out. You know that. This is why it would be a conflict of interest for you to be on the case. You can't go investigating your own dad's alibi."

Alibi? Is he seriously looking into my dad's whereabouts? I had a million thoughts racing in circles around my brain. Suddenly, the thoughts came to a screeching halt. "Wait a second. My dad was in the hospital the entire time I was going to those 911 hang ups. He had knee surgery."

"If he was really in the hospital during the entire time of death window, then I could probably get you put back on the case come Monday. All I have to do is talk to a couple people at the hospital and check some surveillance footage."

"But Monday is too long!" I argued. It was Friday and I didn't want to wait the entire weekend. I wasn't even allowed to call Ryan in response to his letter. "You know, I found a letter from Michelle's son last night. He said he had information that could help our investigation and he specifically wrote to me."

Matt agreed that this was a key piece of information and we should not wait until Monday to contact Ryan. He asked for the phone number so that he could follow up with Ryan that weekend. "Take the weekend off. Trust me, I'm going to handle this. Come Monday, you could be back on this case. Taking a few days off could do you some good."

For some reason, I trusted every word Matt spoke. Maybe he was right. I still needed to break the news to my dad that his secret had been outed since I'd found the photograph of the four of us at Patch Lane. I was hoping Christie would be free for some much-needed girls' time again after I finished explaining this entire shitshow to my dad.

Patch Lane

Chapter 23

"What's wrong, Sarah?" My dad could tell something was wrong before he even gave me his famous bear hug.

I took a deep breath and shrugged my shoulders. "Oh Dad, I don't even know where to begin with this one."

Without saying another word, my dad headed to the kitchen and came back out with two glasses of wine. I guess the automatic response of pairing alcohol and stress was hereditary. After we both were settled on the couch, I began to explain the whirlwind of chaos that the Patch Lane case had stirred up. I told him about how we found the safe at Patch Lane, and what was inside.

My dad set down his glass of wine and fought hard to hold back his tears when I told him about the photograph Michelle had kept all these years.

"Dad, I finally realize how real what you and Michelle had was. You meant so much to her. I couldn't believe she kept a photograph of us in that little safe with her most important possessions. She considered us family, didn't she?"

My dad nodded his head. "Yeah…and I considered her and Ryan family, too."

"I'm so sorry that everyone had to find out about you and Michelle this way. I know it wasn't something you wanted the world to know."

My dad held up his hand. "Sarah, stop. This isn't your fault. There's no need for you to say sorry. If anyone wants to ask me questions about my relationship with Michelle, then they can go right ahead and ask me."

I prepared to give my dad even worse news. "Dad, I think they're going to ask you about more than just your relationship with Michelle. Because your relationship is only coming to light now, I think they're going to try to rule you out as a suspect." I cringed as the words dripped off my tongue. *A suspect.*

My dad puffed out his chest as he inhaled through his nose. He processed what I had said and slowly nodded. "Yes. Well, I suppose if I were still a cop, I would think the same thing about a long-lost boyfriend coming into the picture."

He tried to stay rational and didn't allow himself to show fear in front of me. He had let me catch a glimpse of sadness, and even regret, but never fear.

I leaned over and gave him a big hug. I whispered, "It's going to be okay, Dad." I felt his body quiver as he shook off his emotions. I released my grasp and added, "Besides, you have a solid alibi the night Michelle was killed because you were at the hospital. They're going to be able to review the video footage and see that right away."

"I'm not so sure I would say that they're going to review the footage that quickly, though. You know how slow those suits can be at times."

Now it was time for the third and final hit. "Well, I actually asked a personal favor for them to expedite clearing you."

My dad interrupted me, "Sarah, don't go pulling favors on my behalf. That isn't going to help clear us if someone knows you're pulling strings to move things along."

"No, Dad, that's not why I asked them to expedite it. I mean, not that I don't care about clearing your name." I was stumbling over my own words. "I got kicked off the case. The only way I can get back on is after they clear your name and determine there's no conflict of interest for me."

My dad ran his fingers through his salt and peppered hair. "Jesus, I'm sorry, Sarah. I never meant…"

"Stop. This isn't your fault either, Dad. This isn't either of our faults. This is just a shitty situation that we are going to get past and move forward with our lives."

My dad's line of sight drifted to the coffee table. "You haven't even touched your drink!" He grabbed my glass of wine and placed it in my hand. We clinked glasses and sipped on our wine, relaxed and talked about how much better Italian reds were than Californian reds.

In the midst of our discussion, my phone rang. "Hey Christie!" I answered. "I was actually just thinking about calling you today. What's up?"

"See! I told you I'm psychic! If you were going to call me then does that mean you're off work tonight by any chance?"

"You are in luck. Yes, I am. What did you have in mind?"

Christie let out a squeal. "Yay! Okay, how about girls' night and movies at my place tonight?"

"I haven't spent much time with Hallie at all this week. Would you mind coming over to my place so I could keep her company for a few hours?" I felt like a terrible pet mom lately. I knew Hallie missed me and I could tell she was getting lonely.

"No problem, girl. I'll see you in about an hour."

I hung up my phone, and before I could tell my dad about my new plans he said, "Go ahead. Don't you worry about me. I'm going to finish off this wine here and sort through some insurance paperwork from my surgery."

I left my dad's and headed straight home. I got myself cleaned up before Christie arrived, and we wasted no time before opening the gallon of ice cream and starting the movie marathon. Christie had never been good at paying attention to movies. She usually talked half the time throughout watching one, and this time was no different.

"So, how's work going?"

I didn't tell Christie about being kicked off the Patch Lane case. I really didn't want to get into the details of why, either. "It's stressful, but it's alright. I feel like I never get to hear what's going on in your life though, Christie. What's new with you?"

"Oh, you know, same shit different day. I need to go get a real job. Burger Finite is good money, but I need to grow up. Jesus, I can't believe we're already twenty-four. You know what I realized the other day?" Christie took a long sip of her wine.

"No, what?" I asked.

"We never had our five-year high school reunion. Well, maybe they did but we weren't invited."

"Can't say I really care. Even if we had one, I'm not so sure I would have gone." I wasn't exactly popular in high school and hated almost every minute of it. I spent most of my time with the punk kids and steered clear from the popular crowd. College was when I really learned to love school.

"Yeah, totally. I wouldn't have gone either. You're the only person I even care about from that school. Anyway, there isn't anything new or exciting with me. You know what's been really annoying me lately, though?"

"What's that?" I asked.

"Every single day that I've gone to Dina's to grab my latte before my shift, there's been this woman there who keeps rambling about the trees watching her. She even grabbed my arm a few days ago and was screaming about those goddamn trees. Now I have to make my own decaf coffee in the morning, which is nothing like Dina's lattes. It's ridiculous that Dina won't just ask this woman to leave. When I mentioned it to her, she said that the woman is a paying customer, so she won't ask her to leave. Is there anything you can do about that? Ugh, Dina's has the absolute best lattes."

My mind shot back to Lu. "By any chance, did this woman smell like cigarette smoke?"

"Oh my god!" Christie exclaimed. "How did you know that? Do you know her?"

I legally couldn't tell Christie about the bottles of medication I'd found in Lu's pantry. "I can't really say, Christie, you know what I mean?"

Christie sighed dramatically and responded, "Ugh, yeah. So, can you fix my problem?"

"I'm going to look into it, but I can't make any promises." When I had some free time, I planned to revisit Lu to try and convince her to go see her doctor. Sadly, it sounded like Lu must have skipped making that follow up appointment after my visit with her.

Christie mumbled, "I just want my freaking latte…"

I was annoyed by her lack of patience with Lu, but I kept my judgements to myself. Or at least I tried to.

Christie immediately read my face and asked, "What? Why am I getting that face?"

My mouth slightly opened, realizing I couldn't get anything by her. "Just be nice, Christie. I know you just want to get in and out with your latte but try to understand that maybe she's just slightly different than you. She's not trying to bother you or anyone else."

Christie rolled her eyes, but not in a mocking way, but rather the way that a child who knows they did something wrong and they're in trouble rolls their eyes. "I know, I know. Thanks, mom."

We eventually continued watching the movie. Even if there is complete silence between us, simply being around Christie makes me relax and forget about work. She has this fun energy about her that makes me just giggle at everything she says. We eventually got out our old high school yearbook and began guessing what career path each of our classmates had taken since graduation.

Christie started, "Oh, I bet if we see Dusty at our ten-year reunion, he's going to show up with two toy poodles and be a fashion designer."

I went next. "I bet when Kristen shows up, she's going to be CEO of some company in Pittsburgh."

Christie added to my prediction, "Oh yeah! And I bet she'll come to the reunion in a pink pantsuit, too!"

We laughed hysterically at the mental images our silly speculating had generated. We were still giggling well into the night until we finished our ice cream and slowly drifted to sleep.

Chapter 24

I joined Saturday night's roll call, but on the inside, I missed working the sporadic hours I'd grown accustomed to. It's not that I hated working night shift, but I missed the thrill of focusing my time and energy into one big case and unraveling every clue and piece of evidence like a puzzle.

I got back into the groove of things, making a few traffic stops early in my shift. I got a message from Tim asking if I wanted to meet him in the rear parking lot of the local bank. That was Tim's smoking spot, since Chief Fox wanted his officers to maintain a professional appearance and didn't want anyone smoking in public where we could be seen. Since the bank was obviously closed at night and had nothing but shrubbery behind its rear lot, Tim had dubbed the area his own private smoking spot.

Tim pulled out his cigarette pack and tapped it against his palm three times. As I watched him, I said, "You know, I never understood why smokers always do that."

"Do what?" Tim asked.

"Hit the pack against their palm before they take a cigarette out. Like, is there some secret society of smokers that tells you before you smoke, you have to do that?"

Tim laughed at my naivety. "I wish it was that exciting or cool. No, we tap it to pack as much of the tobacco towards the butt as possible so that it's nice and tight and burns more evenly and slowly."

"Does it really make that much of a difference?"

Tim lit his cigarette, held it up to his mouth for a long inhale, and shrugged his shoulders. "Hell, I have no idea. I guess it's just something I've done for so many years, I don't even remember what the difference would be like if I didn't do it." Tim redirected the conversation, "So, how are you holding up?"

"I'm fine."

"Hastings, you're a tough chick, but I know you're going through some shit right now. I know you're pissed at me for making you tell Sarge about your dad's relationship with Michelle, but I hope you understand I was only trying to help you from making the situation worse."

I had no idea that Tim thought I was mad at him. "Shit, Tim, I'm not pissed at you. You were definitely right. I was thinking irrationally by not telling anyone because I was still dealing with the shock myself. Besides, I know for a fact that if you didn't make me tell, Sloan would have kicked me off the case regardless."

Tim quickly exhaled the smoke he was holding so that he could ask, "Wait, what do you mean kicked off the case? Did they kick you off?"

"Yeah, you didn't hear? In a department this small, I thought everyone would have known by now. Technically my dad is a suspect now, so I have a definite conflict of interest. Sloan seems to think that as soon as they clear my dad, I should be able to get back on the case."

Tim shook his head. "Damn, that sucks."

"Yeah. It actually really sucks a lot. Screw it, can I bum a cig off you?" Tim handed me one out of his pack. I teased, "What? You're not gonna smack it for me first?"

"It's still good from when I packed them before!"

We both laughed and I enjoyed feeling the nicotine race through my bloodstream. Caffeine can only do so much. I was enjoying the last few puffs of my cigarette when Dispatch got on the air.

"Dispatch to 1045."

Tim pressed his mic and responded, "1045, go."

"Respond to 357 Fiddle Lane to speak with the caller regarding suspicious activity at her neighbor's house. The caller stated that her neighbor's home is supposed to be vacant, but she saw someone walking around inside the house."

Since I was already with Tim, I offered to back him up. "1034 to Dispatch, you can add me to 1045's call."

Dispatch responded, "Received."

I followed Tim down to Fiddle Lane and he stopped at a fork in the road. There was a stone sign sitting alongside the path to the left that read "The Shulls," and there was a wooden hanging sign above the path to the right that read "The Lucketts."

Tim got on the radio. "1045 to Dispatch, can you confirm the name of our caller?"

After approximately thirty seconds, Dispatch got on the air. "1045, your caller's name was Lisa Shull."

Tim turned to the left and I followed. We parked our cruisers and walked up the wooden porch steps, opened the screen door, and knocked. A woman came to the door and greeted us.

"Hello, Officers! Thank you so much for coming. Please, come inside."

Tim and I entered the home as we introduced ourselves. "I'm Officer Briggs. This is my partner, Officer Hastings. Can you tell us about your neighbor's house and what happened earlier?"

"Yes. So, our neighbors, the Lucketts, passed away a few years ago. Mr. Luckett has been gone maybe seven or so years and Mrs. Luckett followed only a year or two after that. Their house is supposed to be vacant, but I saw someone inside walking around a few hours ago."

I said, "It appears that the Luckett's farm is a little ways down the road and through the woods from you. What were you doing by their house tonight?"

"Our dog, Lucy, didn't come when I called her earlier. I was worried she ran off chasing a rabbit and wandered too far. She does that sometimes, you know; she's a border collie, so she has a ton of energy and sometimes wanders out too far. I was over there looking and calling for her. When I saw someone inside the house I left and immediately came back home. Thank God, Lucy returned about twenty minutes later. Of course, she had a few blood stains on her fur, which leads me to believe she caught a rabbit or squirrel." Lisa huffed in annoyance and glared down at Lucy, who was laying in the corner of the kitchen.

Tim then asked, "And how exactly are you sure that the house is supposed to be vacant?"

"The Lucketts left their land and home to their son, who lives in Boston. He was here one day and stopped over to speak with us. We've known Jacob since we moved here. I think he was in middle school around that time. Anyway, he stopped by to say hello and told us he was going to keep the land but allow local farmers to use it for crops and hay for a fee. In the end, the money he gets from the farmers pays the property taxes, so he's able to keep it as a future option for when he's ready to settle down. We tried to make him a more than fair offer on the land so that we could expand our farm, but he declined. He did promise to come to us first, though, if he ever decided to sell the property."

"Did you check to make sure that Jacob didn't come back without your knowledge?" Tim asked.

"Oh, that wasn't Jacob in that house. Jacob is an attractive young man. The guy I saw walk past the window was older and had a beard. I can assure you that was not Jacob in that house."

We asked her for additional details about the man she saw. She advised it was an older white male with a beard, average weight. She was unable to provide any more specifics due to her distance from the house. Tim and I looked at each other and silently agreed that we had all the information we needed.

I said, "Thank you very much for your time, Lisa. We are going over to check it out. Stay here and we'll stop back if we need additional information from you."

Lisa thanked us and walked us back to our cruisers. We drove back down the gravel lane and made the sharp turn at the fork in the road. We shut off the lights on our cruisers and moved at a crawling speed until we could see the house in the distance. We parked, got out of our cruisers, and continued on foot.

As we approached the brick ranch-style house, we saw a small lamp illuminating through the window and a man moving in the soft light. I walked around to the rear of the house while Tim approached the front door. Tim knocked hard and bellowed, "Amber Forest Police Department, come to the front door!"

We immediately heard someone run across the floor towards the back of the house. The rear door flew open, slamming into the brick exterior as a male jumped over the three steps and began sprinting away. I ran after the suspect towards the tree line, using the radio as I did so.

"1034, I'm in a foot pursuit! Suspect is running towards the tree line!"

My radio went off repeatedly, but I was too engrossed in my foot pursuit to respond to anyone. I followed the suspect into the woods and was closing the distance between us. I kept sprinting and got close enough that I could just barely reach out to touch him. I dug deep and pushed myself even more, and I was able to grab his shirt and shove him to the ground. I reached around, scooped up his right arm, and bent it behind his back while I slapped my handcuffs on him. Once he was secured, I shifted my weight on his legs and rolled him on to his side, so as not to suffocate him. The entire pursuit was probably less than thirty seconds long, but the way I was panting made it feel like nearly ten minutes.

Tim ran up to us. "Who the hell are you?" he asked our suspect as he bent over, trying to catch his breath.

The suspect spit on Tim's boot and grunted, "Screw you, pigs."

We picked him up and took him back to our cruisers. While we were walking, I updated Dispatch, "1034, we have one in custody."

Before Tim placed the suspect in his cruiser, he searched the suspect for any weapons on his person. He turned the suspect towards the trunk of his cruiser, holding the suspect by his handcuffs, and pressed his knee into the back of the man's leg, that way if the offender tried anything Tim could buckle him to his knees. As he continued his search, he felt the outline of a gun in the man's waistline.

"How many more guns do you have?" Tim asked, pulling out a handgun.

The suspect remained silent.

"Alright, you want to play it that way?" Tim slammed the suspect's face against his cruiser and shoved his knee deeper into the man's leg, pinning him against the trunk. If the offender had a second weapon on him, Tim wanted to make sure he wasn't going anywhere. He finished the search but didn't find anything else.

I took the gun and unloaded it before placing it into an evidence bag and securing it in my cruiser. Sergeant Oakley and Peterson arrived and stayed on scene to process any additional evidence.

I followed Tim to the station and helped him take our suspect into the interrogation room. We handcuffed him to the table and shackled his feet. I grabbed a mobile AFIS and attempted to identify our suspect. I rolled his index finger across the device and waited for the results.

Processing...
Processing...
WANTED
Joseph Walter Muller
Date of Birth: 06/30/1950

Chapter 25

"How the hell did you find him?" Matt raced to the station after he heard we found Joseph. I couldn't tell if he was genuinely excited or if he was partially angry that I had found Joseph while I was kicked off the case.

"A neighbor knew that the house Joseph was staying in was supposed to be vacant, so when she saw someone inside, she called us. It was pure luck and coincidence, I swear."

Matt looked at me suspiciously. "You sure do have an awful lot of coincidences happen to you, don't you?" He added, "Well, I spent my entire day reviewing video footage from the hospital where your dad was at, and I was able to definitively eliminate him as a suspect. I submitted my findings to the FBI agent in charge of the case, and he will have to talk to the U.S. Attorney to officially rule that you are no longer a conflict of interest and can be put back on the case."

"That was so much faster than I thought, thank you so much!" I couldn't believe Matt had investigated my dad so quickly.

"Well, don't thank me yet. It isn't final until the U.S. Attorney gives his stamp of approval."

I hesitatingly asked, "Am I allowed to interview Joseph?"

Matt shook his head. "No, I'm going to have to handle all of that. We're technically arresting him based on his ATF warrants. We still need more evidence before we can pin him for Michelle's murder. Lucky for us, the ATF charges he's facing are pretty hefty and should keep him confined while we can get enough to also get him for Michelle's murder."

I headed to our evidence room to log the gun that we'd found on Joseph. One of the first things we do when we recover firearms is run the serial number through our NCIC database system to make sure that it wasn't stolen. I took the gun out of the bag and turned it on one side, then the other. There was no serial number. This gun looked just like the ones in the old root cellars at Patch Lane. There was no trace that a serial number was ever on the gun.

I told Matt about the gun before logging it into evidence. We both wondered if there was a chance Joseph hid additional guns at this other house. It didn't make much sense, though. Why would Joseph do something so risky and live in a house that was owned by someone else? He could have been caught at any time.

Matt stopped himself in the middle of our conversation. "I actually can't keep talking about this with you. I'm really sorry, Sarah, but it would be jeopardizing my career to discuss the details while you're still off the case. You understand, right?"

I was upset that I wasn't being included in any aspect of the case anymore, even after I'd helped catch Joseph. I really wanted to sit in on the interview with him. "I understand. I don't like it, but I understand."

Matt promised me that as soon as I got reinstated on the case, he would include me. He added, "Listen, if you want to watch the interview from the video room, you're free to do that."

"Alright, I'll do just that." I headed down to the video surveillance room and took a seat.

Joseph sat in the room with his hands cuffed to the table and his feet shackled to the floor. Matt entered the room, followed by Tim.

"Mr. Muller, I am U.S. Deputy Marshal Sloan. Officer Tim Briggs is here to serve as a witness. I want to ask you a few questions." Matt continued by reading Joseph his rights and asking a few general questions. Then Matt dove into the real questioning. "So, Joseph. What were you doing at that house?"

Joseph sat in silence with anger across his face.

"No response? Alright. Let's talk about how you've been on the run for nearly twenty years. Where have you been all this time?"

Still no response from Joseph.

Matt was growing annoyed with Joseph and decided to leave the room to get the gun I had logged as evidence. He returned and slammed it on the table. "You want to explain the shitty job you did at filing off the serial numbers from this gun?"

Joseph grew angrier and finally spoke. "The only shitty job being done here is by you."

Matt responded, "I just want to understand what the hell could have possibly been going through your head. I mean, you're really a goddamn idiot. You could have fled this town, hell, you could have fled this country. But instead you chose to stay, and if that wasn't stupid enough, you chose to go crash at somebody else's house? Even if it was vacant, surely you knew that someone else owned it and you'd be caught."

Joseph snapped, "I'm not a goddamn idiot. I just stopped giving a shit. I have stage four prostate cancer and I stopped giving a shit about whether or not I was caught. You know what, I want my lawyer. I'm done talking to you, *pig*."

Joseph had said the magic "L" word. Matt stormed out of the interrogation room and I could hear him swearing. Tim quietly followed suit. Matt eventually asked Tim to move Joseph back into his jail cell rather than waiting on his lawyer.

I glanced down at my watch and saw it was already 0630 hours. I was ready to unrack my cruiser and head home to Hallie.

Patch Lane

Chapter 26

I was about half an hour into Sunday night's shift when I remembered Christie's request that I follow up with Lu, so she could go back to getting her lattes from Dina's in peace. It was nearly midnight, but I also remembered Lu told me that she was up all hours of the night. I figured it wouldn't hurt to swing by Chip Lane and see if any lights were on inside her house.

As I pulled up to Lu's driveway, she was sitting on her porch puffing away at a cigarette. I parked my cruiser and waved as I walked toward her, so she knew I came in peace. "Hi, Lu. How are you doing tonight?"

She exhaled a smoke cloud and responded, "Hello, Officer Hastings! I'm good, real good. Did I call you? I don't remember calling you."

"Oh no, I'm actually here to check in on you and see how you're doing. I heard you've been very concerned about the trees watching you. Did you get to see Dr. Boyd last week?"

Lu looked off to the side. "I didn't have time to see Dr. Boyd. She's busy with other people around the town calling up, calling her down, they just all run around and around."

Lu had clearly not been taking her medication. She tended to become more disorganized the more excited or anxious she became.

"Well, I think it would really be good for you to see Dr. Boyd this week. I'm worried about you, Lu. I can tell that you are very upset because you feel that the trees are watching you."

Lu put out her cigarette and grew louder. "They *are* watching me! I'll show you!"

To my surprise, Lu hopped up out of her seat and started down the stairs. I could tell she was on a mission. I let her continue, because I thought if she could show me exactly what was upsetting her, I might be able to better help her. I mentally ran through a few scenarios of what it could be; an owl, a bird in its nest, or several other animals that could be sitting in the trees "watching" her.

Lu hurried down her driveway as I followed. She suddenly stopped and turned around. "Hold on! I need my sun."

I wasn't sure what Lu meant by that, but she ran into her house and bent over to grab something that was sitting on the floor next to the door. She came back outside with a handheld spotlight. She added, "Now we can go around and up the trees, you'll see with the sun."

I followed Lu towards the woods along the back of her property. We walked for at least five minutes before the shadowy oaks stood large and towered above us. Lu turned on her spotlight and shined it up into the branches. "There! You see it! That's where it's watching me."

Well I'll be damned. There was an old, wooden treehouse built high into one of the sturdy oaks. It wasn't a large structure, just a single room that could probably fit no more than a couple middle schoolers at a time. It had to be at least twenty-five feet off the ground, and with so many surrounding trees, it made for a well-camouflaged perch.

"I see the treehouse, Lu. Are you saying that someone sits up there and watches you?"

Lu got excited that I was finally validating her claims. "Yes! Exactly! He's God. He watches over everything and he is in the tree, you'll see him day and night, but usually at night."

"Okay, I understand. How about if I go check it out tomorrow and see if I can get him to stop watching you?"

Lu smiled as she replied, "Thank you, Officer Hastings, that would be really great!"

I added, "And in return, can you do me a favor and see Dr. Boyd one day this week?"

Lu glanced down at her feet and kicked a rock a short distance. "Yeah, Officer, I guess I can do that."

I walked Lu back to her house, ensured she was safely inside, and reminded her to lock her doors at night, even though she was on a private farm. She agreed, and I got back inside my cruiser to finish the rest of my shift. I headed back down Chip Lane and turned right onto the main road. As I followed Route 86 around the bend, I passed Patch Lane. I wondered if the treehouse was actually on Patch Lane's property. I drove a little farther down the road and pulled into a store parking lot. I reached into my glove box and dug around for an Amber Forest map. Once I found it, I unfolded it and spread it out on my lap.

Luckily, since Amber Forest was less than fifty square miles, the map was fairly detailed. I found Patch Lane on the map and drew an X approximately where the farmhouse sat on the property. Then, I found Chip Lane and marked where I thought Lu's house sat on her property. The two farms didn't sit like square blocks of land, one behind the other, like I'd originally thought. Instead they were adjacent, triangular shaped properties—meeting at one tip—with another farm fitting in between them like a third piece of pie. The three properties together completed a large, half-circle of land. I followed the third slice of property to the nearest road and saw it sat on Peachtree Lane.

I scribbled the road name in my notepad and placed it back into my front vest pocket. I decided to wait until morning to call Matt and suggest we check out this third farm. If there really was a mystery guy spying on Lu, there was a chance that he had a good view of the Patch Lane farm as well. Even though I was still kicked off the Patch Lane case, it seemed like I was constantly being drawn right back into the eye of the storm. Rose's words rolled through my mind. *She was immediately drawn to the house, like a moth to a flame.*

Patch Lane

152

Chapter 27

I was so anxious to call Matt on Monday morning that as soon as my shift ended at 0700 hours, I dialed his number.

"Hello?" Matt answered.

"Hey Matt, it's Sarah. I got some interesting information I wanted to run past you. Are you free to meet up?"

"I just woke up, so I can meet you in an hour or two. Will you be home or at the station?"

I was going to wait at the station to talk to Matt, but if he was going to take nearly two hours then I decided I'd rather go home and unwind first. "I'm finishing my shift up now, so are you able to swing by my place then?"

"No problem. See you in a bit." Matt hung up and I headed home.

Hallie was excited to see me and demanded that I give her attention before I was allowed to undress. I removed my duty belt and vest and set them in their usual spot on the chair in the corner of my bedroom. I stripped off my uniform and laid the clothes in a pile in the corner to deal with after I got some sleep. Hallie took advantage of my laziness and nestled on my clothes, curling up into the tiniest, cutest little ball of fur.

By the time I'd showered, got dressed, and made some food, two hours had quickly passed. Matt knocked on my front door right as I set my dirty dishes in the sink. I walked over and opened my door to let him inside. He stood in the doorway with a big smile on his face, and I could tell he had something exciting to share.

"I have some good news," he announced.

"Yeah?" I invited him inside to talk.

"Well, I told you how I was able to clear your dad, so I forwarded my findings to our FBI guy handling the case and I asked him to submit an urgent request to the U.S. Attorney to officially rule that you are exempt as a conflict of interest. I told him you've been like a partner on this case, since Jackson had to go on leave since his wife went into labor. He agreed and sent the memo over the weekend. I woke up this morning to confirmation that the U.S. Attorney approved your reinstation."

"Holy shit!" I couldn't hide my excitement, not that I tried. "That's amazing! Thank you so much for everything you did to push it forward."

Matt shook his head and held up his right hand. "No, no. Thank *you*. You have been essential to this case and helped me out in ways even Jackson couldn't have been able to if he were still here."

I had never been good at accepting compliments. "Let's just call it even and say we make a damn good team. Do you have any updates on Joseph? Did you ever look into the owner of the house on Fiddle Lane that Joseph was hiding in?"

"Well, now that you're officially back on the case I'm happy to discuss all of those details with you. I wish I had something more exciting to share, but that turned out to be a dead end. Joseph lawyered up, as you saw, and hasn't talked since. We contacted Jacob Luckett, and as the neighbors said, he lives in Boston. He visits Amber Forest about twice a year to check on the property, but for the most part he just has some farmers take care of the land, and in return they get all the hay they want. As for the house, he said he keeps it indefinitely winterized. He doesn't want to sell it, but also doesn't plan to move back here for at least another five years or so. He has a great job in Boston working as a Chief Compliance Officer for some company."

"Those guys make some serious money. Can't blame him for not wanting to move back to Amber Forest."

Matt agreed and asked, "So what did you originally call me here to discuss?"

I was so excited about being back on the case that I'd forgotten I was the one who asked Matt to come by in the first place. "Oh, right! I was talking to the resident who lives on the Chip Lane farm, and long story short, she showed me a treehouse on her neighbor's farm that she believes someone watches her from. She suffers from at least one mental illness, so it was hard to get many details from her, but I think this treehouse could potentially have a view of the Patch Lane farm, too. I want to go take a look and find out what exactly we can see from that treehouse."

"Wow. That sounds pretty interesting. I'm definitely on board with that idea. I see you couldn't keep your brain off the case this weekend, huh?"

"Yeah, I guess you could say that." What I wanted to say was that I felt like this case was following *me*, rather than the other way around. I asked, "Did you ever follow up with Michelle's son, Ryan?"

"No. I was so focused on trying to get you put back on the case as soon as possible that I didn't get a chance to talk to Ryan. Looks like we have two big things to follow up on today. You said you worked all night, right?"

I was upset that Matt had broken his promise and didn't talk to Ryan, but I couldn't ignore that the reason was because he was trying to help me. *How mad can I be at someone who broke a promise so they could help me?* I answered Matt's last question, "Yeah, why? Do I look that bad?"

Matt laughed. "No, I only meant you must be running on fumes. Why don't you get some sleep, and I'll try to track Ryan down and see if he's free for a phone call this afternoon."

"That sounds like a good plan to me. If I get four or five hours of sleep, I'll be good."

Chapter 28

I got my five hours of sleep and started my morning with a pot of coffee. I called Matt to let him know that I was awake and would be ready to go within the hour. I cleaned up, got dressed, and poured my coffee in a to-go mug.

I met Matt at the station and we both headed up to Chief Fox's office to let him know that I was approved by the U.S. Attorney to be back on the case. We approached his office and saw he was on the phone. I gently knocked on his open door. He held up one finger, then waved us both inside.

"Absolutely. I couldn't agree more. I can promise you we will do our best to help keep your children safe. I'll follow up with you next week, Mrs. Cooper. Mhm, goodbye." Chief Fox hung up the phone and stood up. "Deputy Sloan, pleasure to see you. Sorry about that, we've been getting an influx of complaints about people speeding on Trout Camp Run Road ever since they built the new Dollar Plus store." Chief Fox reached out his arm and shook Matt's hand. "Officer Hastings." I got a simple nod. "What brings you two in here today?"

Matt spoke first. "I wanted to let you know that since I was able to rule out Officer Hastings' father as a suspect, the U.S. Attorney officially ruled that she is no longer considered a conflict of interest in the Patch Lane case."

Chief Fox cleared his throat. "Ah, I see. Well, if the U.S. Attorney makes a ruling, who am I to disagree? Is there anything else?"

"I believe that's all," Matt responded as he began to leave Chief Fox's office.

Chief Fox added, "Officer Hastings, can I have a moment? Privately?"

Matt gave me an *Only God can help you here* look and closed the door behind him.

"Yes, sir?" I asked.

"I don't know who the hell you think you are, going above my head like that. If I pull you off a case, then I pull you off the goddamn case. This is not the time or place to show off your girl power. I can't go and tell Deputy Sloan to revoke this decision, but I want you to know this, Hastings: I have my eye on you. And don't think for a minute that I won't fire you for disobeying an order. You hear me?"

"Yes, sir." I should have expected this response from Chief Fox.

"Now get the hell out of my office."

After I left, I found Matt waiting for me by the stairwell. He asked, "So, how bad did he let you have it?"

I took a deep breath and answered, "It could have been worse."

"Alright, let's go see Ryan, then."

"Wait, see him? I thought we were going to call him. Doesn't he live in Maryland?" I wasn't prepared for a road trip to Maryland right then.

Matt laughed. "We got lucky. I called him and it turns out he is in town at his Great Grandma's this week."

He must have been staying at Rose's. *Shoot*, I still had the coffee mug she'd given me. "Do we have time to swing by my place before we go there?"

"Yeah, we should have time. You forget something?"

"Yeah. Thanks."

Matt pulled up to my apartment and waited in the car while I ran inside to grab the coffee mug. When I returned, he noticed it in my hand.

"You forgot an empty coffee mug?" Matt asked.

"Yeah, I was actually at Rose's the other night for a 911 hang up call. She let me borrow her mug and I promised I would bring it back to her."

Matt was about to put his car in drive, but stopped and threw the shifter back into park. "Whoa, you were with Michelle's grandmother and didn't tell me? What happened there? Who called 911?"

Shit, I'm in trouble now. "It turned out to be some crossed wires or something." *Or something.* "I got to talking to Rose and I realized during our conversation that she was Michelle's grandmother. She told me a lot of interesting things about Michelle. Did you know about her, um, special skill?"

Matt raised one eyebrow. "That depends on which special skill you're talking about."

"I'm not going to play this stupid game. Did you know she was psychic?" I wasn't sure why I was being short with Matt.

"Yes. Well, I know that's the story at least. I don't believe in that stuff."

I suddenly realized why I was irritated with Matt. He knew this key piece of information about Michelle and never told me. My tone grew colder. "I didn't believe in it either until I spoke with Rose. I'm not sure how you can be upset with me for speaking with her and finding out a piece of information about Michelle—one that you already knew and didn't tell me."

Matt shifted the car into drive. "When I first started on this case, I had no idea how involved and how crucial you would end up being in it. Usually the local cops just help us out here and there, so we don't give them an entire case file on our subjects. I really didn't think the story about her being psychic was relevant anyways."

The car ride to Rose's was quiet. As we pulled into her driveway, Matt commented on her log home. "You don't see many log homes anymore. I always liked the smell of my parents' log cabin at the lake. Something very soothing about the smell of natural wood."

We approached her front door and Rose greeted us with a big smile. "Officer Hastings! It's such a pleasure to see you again. And who is this with you today?" She glanced to my left at Matt.

He extended his hand and introduced himself. "Hello, I'm Deputy Matthew Sloan with the U.S. Marshals. Feel free to call me Matt."

Rose gently shook his hand and held onto it while she asked, "Did you know my granddaughter, Michelle?"

"No ma'am, I'm sorry I did not have the pleasure of knowing her. I work out of the Pittsburgh district and have been assigned to investigate her murder."

I could tell that the word *murder* shook Rose. I handed her the coffee mug and thanked her for letting me borrow it.

"Oh, no problem at all. Thank you for everything that you do."

We followed Rose inside, and a young man walked out of the kitchen. "Hi, I'm Ryan. You must be Officer Hastings and Deputy Sloan."

We all sat down at the dining table and watched as Ryan set some papers on the table. "Thank you for following up with my letter. I had some things I wanted to show you in person," Ryan began saying.

Before he continued, I interrupted with an apology. "I'm really sorry it took us so long to get back to you. Somehow your letter was stuck at our assistant's desk. I'm just glad we got lucky and found out that you were in town."

Ryan responded, "Oh yeah, I've been coming home a lot more often because I'm trying to find a job in Pittsburgh. I don't mind the two-hour drive to the city for an interview. I like to stay here, and I always try to spend an extra day or two with my gram. I'm not sure if you've noticed, but she's a pretty cool chick."

Rose laughed at Ryan's sense of humor and added, "Yeah, I guess I am a cool chick, huh?"

I smiled at Rose and Ryan's relationship, thinking about how sweet they both were.

Ryan continued, "Anyways, I wanted to show you both this letter I received only a week before my mom died." He pushed a handwritten letter across the table to Matt and me. The neatly formed writing read:

Dear Ryan,

I cannot imagine the pain, both physically and mentally, that you are currently enduring. I wish I could be there to hold your hand while you fight the hardest battle of your life. Please know that your mother never stopped loving you and would do anything to be there with you.

For your safety, keep this letter close to your heart and do not tell or show it to anyone.

Love you forever,

Mom

Matt and I stared blankly at each other, letting the words sink in. It was Matt who had the courage to ask the obvious question. "Ryan, what battle is your mom referring to?"

Ryan's eyes opened wide as he shrugged and answered, "That's the thing! I have no idea! I'm doing well, I'm healthy, I'm in no pain. I honestly have no idea what she was talking about. I held onto this letter for about a week and I didn't know what to do with it. She told me not to tell anyone, so I didn't. I wasn't even sure if it was actually real or if it was some sick hoax. Then, when I heard about her death…her *real* death, I still didn't know what to make of this letter. I eventually decided to tell you guys about it in case it could help."

I held the letter in my hands and slowly read it over and over again. "Ryan, this is a pretty big piece of evidence. It almost sounds like she thought you were dying. Do you have any idea why she thought that?"

"Around the same time, I got this letter, one of my friends told me that he'd found an online fundraiser for me. When I looked up the page, I saw it was someone pretending to be a friend of mine saying that I had cancer and they were raising money for my medical bills. I contacted the website directly and they took the page down after a few days. I don't know why this rumor ever started. I thought someone was playing a prank on me. Here, you can see for yourself." Ryan handed us a few printed screenshots from the website that no longer existed.

"Did you ever hear from your mom again?"

"No, I never did. This letter was the only thing I heard from her. Do you think it was really my mom?" Ryan's eyes began filling with tears. He fought as hard as he could to hold them back from falling down his cheeks and pursed his lips together to hold in his vocal cries.

I let Matt handle this one. He responded, "I can't say for certain, but I do think it's very possible your mom snuck this one by us and mailed you this letter. As you know, she was in our Witness Protection Program, so she wasn't allowed to contact you for both her safety and yours. I'm really sorry this happened to her, Ryan."

Ryan sniffled, coughed, then spoke in a deep tone as an attempt to hide his emotions. "Yeah, thanks. I just want to find the son of a bitch who did this to my mom. I heard you caught the guy that caused her to go into hiding. Do you think he killed her?"

"It's too early to say, but it's looking more and more like he could be our guy." I could tell Matt was not happy with my answer.

He tried to correct my response, adding, "Like Officer Hastings said, it's too early to tell."

We thanked Ryan for contacting us and I wished him luck on all his future job interviews. Matt and I left and began driving towards the station. We approached a T-intersection and Matt asked, "It's still daylight, you want to go check out that treehouse now?"

"Hell yeah. Let's go!" I was excited since I thought we would have spent more time at Rose's and didn't think we were going to have time to do both follow ups in the same day. Matt made the right turn at the intersection and started towards the direction of Patch Lane.

Matt asked, "So which property has the treehouse?"

"Peachtree Lane. It's up here on the left. You'll make a left, and then another, I think." I pulled out my map to be sure. "Yeah. Okay. I'll let you know when to turn."

I relayed the directions to Matt and when we arrived, we found three houses sitting on Peachtree Lane. I had to pull out my map again to try and figure out which house was connected to the property that faced Lu's home and the house on Patch Lane. "I think it's the second one on the right," I directed Matt.

We approached the house and knocked on the door. No answer. Matt knocked again and identified himself as a Deputy U.S. Marshal. Out of the corner of my eye, I saw someone peek through the blinds on the lower level window. Within seconds, the blinds returned to normal and we heard footsteps approaching the front door. A small, meek man poked his head out and greeted us in the form of a question, "Hello?" He looked a little older than my dad, possibly in his sixties.

"Hello sir, I'm Officer Hastings with the Amber Forest Police Department, and this is Deputy Sloan with the U.S. Marshals. Do you, by chance, own the property sitting directly behind your home?"

"Yes. Is there something wrong?" The man began to subtly rock sideways against the front door.

"No, sir. We were just wondering if the treehouse in the woods belonged to you?"

The man nervously answered, "Yes. Yes, it does."

"What's your name, sir? Again, you're not in any trouble here." I didn't want to startle the man, who was already growing anxious.

"Martin. Martin Agnew."

"It's nice to meet you, Martin. Would you mind if we came in to ask you a few questions?"

"No, ma'am. Please, come in." Martin opened the door and let us inside. He directed us to his family room and moved some blankets and papers off his couch to make room for us to sit down. "Here you go, please, have a seat."

Matt and I sat down. I asked, "So, Martin, who uses that treehouse?"

Martin glanced down to the floor. "Oh, I don't know, no one really, I guess."

"Does anyone else live here?"

"No, not since my mother died a few years ago." Martin fidgeted, picking at his fingers and rocking slightly back and forth. His demeaner made me wonder if he was on the autism spectrum. I learned in my CIT training course that individuals who are high on the spectrum could appear to be what most people view as socially awkward and may have subtle physical ticks, such as rocking.

"So, you live here alone now. Do you work?" I asked.

"No, I'm retired."

"Oh really? What did you do when you worked?"

"I worked on the phone lines. If someone's phone stopped working, I would go out and fix it."

I instantly thought of Scooter. What if Martin was my 911 hang up caller? I jotted down my theory on my notepad and subtly showed it to Matt.

Matt chimed in and asked, "Martin, would you mind showing us the treehouse?"

Martin drew his brows together, tilted his head, and responded, "Yeah, sure, but I'm kind of confused about why you're so concerned about my treehouse? What's going on?"

I handled this one. "We got a report from a concerned neighbor saying that she was being watched by someone in your treehouse. If it was you, we aren't going to arrest you, but we're going to advise you to stop observing your neighbors in this manner, in order to keep the peace."

Martin became highly agitated. "Well, I never said I was in that treehouse!"

"I know, Martin, I know," I assured him soothingly. "But we'd like to take a look at the treehouse and make sure you can actually see into your neighbor's house from it. If we find that we don't have a clear view past the trees, then we can chalk it up to a mistake and forget about all this completely."

"Alright...I guess that makes sense." Martin grabbed his raincoat and headed outside. "They're calling for rain, you know. Better safe than sorry."

We followed Martin into the woods and walked for approximately ten minutes before we finally got to the treehouse. Martin pointed up and said, "Well, here it is."

"Do you mind if we go up?" Matt asked.

"Sure. It's not very big, though, we can't all fit. You might want to go one at a time."

Matt volunteered to go first. Rectangular pieces of lumber nailed to the tree trunk made up a makeshift ladder. I watched him ascend slowly and carefully until he reached the treehouse above, easily twenty-five feet above ground. He briefly disappeared into the treehouse before poking his head out the window. He spent about a minute in the treehouse before he made his way back down to solid ground.

Matt's cheeks were flushed and there was an energized excitement in his expression. "Sarah, go check that out. Let me know what you think." He was clearly intrigued by what he saw.

I climbed my way up the ladder and into the treehouse. The floorboards creaked so loudly under my weight that I feared they were going to snap. It seemed so much higher once I was up there, and it didn't comfort me when I detected a mild swaying of the structure. I looked closely at the floorboards to make sure they would hold, and that's when I noticed two boards in significantly better condition than the rest. Most of the planks had grayed with age, but these two must have been replaced fairly recently since their yellowish, honey color stood out in contrast.

I cautiously leaned out over the window opening and looked in the direction of Lu's house. Sure enough, I could see it clearly. With a good set of binoculars, I could probably see her sitting on her front porch smoking away like a chimney. I slowly scanned the area and spotted the house on Patch Lane. From this vantage point, I had a good view of the side of the house. I could also see the front door and had a clear sightline into the backyard, including where the entrance to the root cellar would be. At this distance, I would need binoculars to see details such as faces, but the perch definitely afforded a clear visual of both houses.

I climbed back down right as rain was starting to drizzle. I turned to Martin and said, "You were smart to bring your raincoat. How about we head back to your house so we can ask you a few more questions?"

Martin agreed, and the three of us rushed back to the house, trying to beat the rain. We scurried inside and made our way back to the family room just as big drops were starting to fall.

I needed to get Martin to admit that he still used the treehouse. I kept my tone easygoing as I said, "I noticed that a couple of the floorboards were recently replaced in the treehouse. When was that done?"

"Oh, um, I think I did that about a year or so ago." Martin stood up. "Do you mind excusing me while I go use the restroom?"

"By all means, this is your home," I answered.

Martin left the room, heading down the hallway. As soon as he was out of sight, Matt exclaimed, "He has a clear shot of the Patch Lane house. I don't give a shit if he's out there watching that crazy lady. I want to know what he saw go on at Patch Lane. He could be our caller."

I whispered, "I know, I know. I'm thinking the same thing. But he seems a little fragile, so I didn't want to come in too hot. Let me try to ease him into opening up."

Matt agreed to let me take the lead, and we quieted down as we heard Martin making his way back towards the family room. Martin took a seat and asked, "Do either of you need a glass of water? Or a cup of coffee? I'm happy to go put a pot on."

"No, it's alright, Martin. We're both fine, thank you. We just really wanted your help with something," I assured him.

"Oh, alright. I'm happy to help you both in any way I can. I'm a big supporter of law enforcement."

"Thank you, Martin. That's very nice to hear. So, we know you've recently been in the treehouse to replace the boards. I'm sure you've heard the news over the years about the different incidents at the Patch Lane farm—you know, the old Werner Farm."

Martin nodded. "Yes, I've heard. I never liked the man that lived in that house before. Did you guys really catch Joseph Muller?"

"Yes, we caught him." Matt responded.

"Are you sure he's going to stay in jail a long time?" Martin asked nervously. I began to suspect that he was afraid of Joseph.

"Yes, we're sure. He's facing several felony charges by the federal government," Matt assured Martin.

I could tell that Martin was slowly letting his guard down. I decided it was a good time to start pushing him for more answers. "Martin, do you like to sit up in your treehouse? It's okay if you lied to us earlier. We're really hoping you can help us. We need you to be honest with us right now."

Martin slowly inhaled and held his breath. He finally released and answered embarrassedly, "Yes, ma'am. I'm sorry. I just don't want to be in any trouble."

"It's okay. Thank you for being honest. You're not in any trouble. Did you see anything suspicious at Patch Lane about a month ago? You know we're investigating a murder there, right?" I hoped he would admit to watching over the Patch Lane property and give us some type of clue.

"Yeah…I know." Martin took another deep breath in an attempt to calm his nerves. "I saw it."

"You saw what?" I asked.

"I saw the murder, ma'am."

Matt and I nearly had to pick our jaws up off the floor. We were not expecting that response from Martin.

Matt blurted out questions as they ran through his head. "Wait, what? You saw the murder? When? How?"

I could see Martin was beginning to feel overwhelmed, so I stopped him before he spoke. "Martin, how about you just tell us exactly what you saw?"

Martin paused, his mental wheels clearly turning. "Okay. It was about three or four nights before you guys found her body. I know when you found her because I remember all of the police lights. I was looking with my binoculars and saw a girl go into the house through the front door. It was only a few minutes later when I saw her body get dragged out of the house around back and down into a cellar."

"Were you able to recognize the guy who was dragging the body? Was it Joseph?"

"No, I didn't. And it wasn't a guy dragging the body, it was a woman."

I had broken the first rule of being a good investigator. I'd assumed something that wasn't a fact. I had been so sure that the murderer was Joseph, that it didn't even occur to me someone else, let alone a woman, could have been our culprit. I asked Martin, "Have you ever seen the woman before? Did you recognize her?"

"No, I hadn't. I really didn't get a good look at her."

"Why didn't you call the police when you saw what happened?" I asked.

Martin apprehensively replied, "Well, I was scared it was related to something Joseph Muller did. I heard he has ties to the mafia. He's not someone you go squealing on. He's been doing shady business for as long as I can remember."

Matt decided to be blunt and asked, "Did you make calls to 911 and hang up?"

"Yeah, that was me. I knew how to do it and still had the old phone from before I retired. I thought it was the best way to remain anonymous. I tried calling several times, but the cops kept leaving the house without finding the body. The second night I called, I thought I could lure you inside by leaving the front door open. It worked, but I didn't realize there was no access to the body from inside at that point. I thought the cellar that the body was dragged into led to the house, but since you didn't find it, I went over to check it out myself. I followed the cellar tunnel and realized it went to a room in the basement, but I couldn't get through to the rest of the house. I went back through the front door and realized why you guys weren't finding the body. It was because of that padlock on the basement door. After that, I went and got my bolt cutters and removed the lock. Then I called 911 again and that time you finally found her."

"Wow. That was very brave of you. We would have never found Michelle Kline if it weren't for you," I praised him, really meaning the words.

Martin's cheeks grew red and he thanked me for the compliment.

I asked, "Did you make any other 911 hang up calls?" All that was left was for him to explain why he called me to Rose's house.

"No, ma'am. At least, not in many years. I made a few about twenty years ago around the time that Joseph disappeared. I saw that he was running guns all over his property, so I would wait until I saw him leave and I kept calling the police from the phone box on the side of the house. They only searched the house, though, and weren't finding the guns. I'm not sure how, but they eventually found some of them. I kept seeing Joseph run around that farm over the years, but I gave up on trying to be the hero. The only reason I called this time was because someone was murdered. I couldn't believe it! That poor woman."

That explained the 911 hang ups that Tim had responded to back when Michelle was still alive. I still wanted to find out if Martin was the reason I responded to Rose's house. Not willing to let it go, I asked, "Did you make a 911 hang up call from Michelle Kline's grandmother's house?"

"No, ma'am. I don't even know who her grandmother is."

I could tell that Martin was telling the truth. *Then who made the 911 hang up call to Rose's house?* Rose seemed to believe her late husband, Samuel, had led me there. I wasn't so quick to assume that ghosts were calling the police, but then that left me wondering who else could have called if it wasn't Martin.

"Martin, if we developed a suspect, would you be able to identify her as the one who dragged Michelle's body into the cellar?"

"No, I'm sorry. I really didn't get a good look at her face. She was mostly hunched over. I could tell it was a woman by her body figure, how she walked, and her long hair that was pulled back. She looked older, like she could be close to my age. Other than that, I can't be of much more help."

What woman would want Michelle dead? Maybe Joseph had a partner or a secret lover, perhaps? I had so many questions, but I decided that Martin had probably answered as many of them as he could, so I turned to Matt and said, "I think we got a lot of solid information here, thanks to Martin. Deputy, do you have anything further before we leave?"

Matt answered, "No, I think you covered everything, Officer Hastings. Martin, we might follow up with you to make an official statement at the station. Would you be alright with that?"

"Yeah, that's no problem."

We each thanked Martin for his time, and he escorted us to the front door. The raindrops from earlier had turned into a full torrential downpour. Matt unlocked the Forester and we both made a run for it.

Matt started driving and his windshield wipers were working double-time. He glanced over at me and said, "Goddamn, that was not what I was expecting."

"Me either."

Chapter 29

Matt told me that he needed to head back to Pittsburgh to have a strategy meeting with the rest of their task force, given all the new information that we had uncovered. He was going to debrief them about Ryan's letter from his mother and the things Martin had witnessed. Matt suggested I take advantage of the day off to try and unwind or do something relaxing. I contemplated whether I wanted to visit my dad or call Christie. Then I realized that in all this chaos, I hadn't seen the one person I always went to when I needed to calm down: my Aunt Maggie.

Aunt Maggie had been there for me all my life, and if anyone could help me sort through this chaos, it was her. I always felt better after speaking with her and spending time on her secluded farm. She had a way of putting things into perspective; between her classic farmhouse, vibrant garden, and acres of nothing but fields, it was the perfect cocktail for relaxation. I spent nearly half of my childhood at her farm while my dad did his best to raise me on his own while working fulltime. I grabbed my phone and dialed her number.

She answered the phone with her sweet, singsong greeting I knew so well, "Helloooo!"

"Hi, Aunt Maggie!"

"Hi, honey. How are you?"

"Can I come and spend tonight with you? I need a mini vacay right now."

"Sure, you know you are *always* welcome in my home."

"Thank you so much! Do you mind if I bring Hallie with me?"

"Hallie? Who's Hallie? Is this a new friend?"

"No, it's my cat I recently adopted."

"Oh, I didn't know you got a cat. Your dad didn't mention anything when we last spoke. I'm looking forward to meeting her. Drive safely and I'll see you soon."

I grabbed some clean clothes from my closet and gathered my toiletries from the bathroom. Packing my things only took ten minutes. It was Hallie's food, bowls, bed, litter box, and supplies that took the most time to collect. Once I had everything ready, I loaded the bags into the car, put Hallie in her new carrier, and headed for Aunt Maggie's. I instantly began to feel my stress level decline. I drove slowly, since the rain was still coming down heavily and some of the local streets were starting to flood. I listened to the radio quietly, mostly focused on the sound of the rain. I opted to take the back roads to Aunt Maggie's house even though it added about seven minutes to the trip.

Aunt Maggie's house was a beautiful and spacious, two-story farmhouse with a wraparound porch. She took great pride in her home and spent countless hours tending to the colorful flower beds that lined the front walkway and drive. As an avid gardener and cook, her vegetable beds were always green and lush. Since I'd arrived later in the day, I wasn't surprised to see her sitting on the front porch working a crossword puzzle and enjoying a cool glass of lemonade while she watched the rain. I knew she was waiting for me to arrive and the gesture made me feel so loved. Once she saw me, she placed her crossword book in a basket and rushed to meet me. It was so nice to see her, and I knew Hallie was ready to get out of her carrier. She'd been meowing for the last ten minutes of the ride. I guess she was afraid of the unknown. I certainly could relate to that.

"Hi, Sarah. How was your trip?"

"It was good. No traffic, which was nice. The rain slowed me down a little bit, but it really wasn't that bad."

"That's good. I was worried you would have to take an alternate route with the flooding starting."

"I took the shade way so that I stayed off the highway and didn't have to worry about the other cars on the road." The "shade way" was my Aunt Maggie's made-up name for the back road between her and my dad's house. It earned this title because of the five miles of large oak trees that provided a nice, shaded route during the hot summer. I remember when I was little, I used to think the name of the road was Shade Way. I bet I was nearly fifteen years old when I realized it was actually a nickname my Aunt Maggie made up.

"Oh, that's smart of you. I always prefer that way myself. It sounds like your new friend would like to get out of the car, so how about we take her inside, and I'll make you dinner. I have stuffed chicken breasts in the oven and green beans on the stove."

As I carried Hallie through the front door, I could smell the chicken, the freshly baked bread resting on the kitchen island, and the faint traces of a homemade peach pie. Oh, how wonderful it was to be there. It reminded me of all the times I would stay with Aunt Maggie as a young child while my dad was working double shifts. Sometimes I really missed those days.

"Sarah, do you mind setting the table? I just need to pull the chicken out of the oven and drain the green beans. Then, everything should be ready to eat."

"Sure, I can handle that. Are the dishes still in the same cupboard?"

"Yes, center section, lower shelf. The silverware is in the drawer beside the refrigerator."

Once I'd finished the chore, I helped Aunt Maggie carry the heavy pots to the table. She made a lot of food for only the two of us, but I guess after so many years of making meals for me and my dad, she couldn't break the habit.

We sat and loaded our plates. Everything smelled delicious and tasted incredible. I didn't realize until the first bite how much I missed my aunt's cooking.

"Everything is delicious! I forgot how amazing your stuffed chicken breasts taste."

"Well thank you, but I can't take all the credit. The butcher shop always gives me the best cuts of meat. That makes the biggest difference when you're cooking."

We enjoyed dinner, and I ate so much food I could hardly move. I helped Aunt Maggie clear the table, load the dishwasher, and put away the leftovers. We then retired to the front porch to enjoy glasses of Riesling and the sound of the rain.

"So, how's work? Are you busy?" she asked.

"Oh, you have no idea. With the murder case I caught last month, things have been crazy. I'll be very happy once things return to normal."

"Oh, are you on that Patch Lane murder case I saw on the news? I'm glad you caught the guy. That jerk was no good from the start. I guess his luck finally ran out."

"Well, we actually don't think that the guy we arrested is the murderer. He definitely was wanted for multiple federal charges stemming from nearly twenty years ago, but we have reason to believe that the murderer was someone else."

"Oh, that's interesting."

Since Aunt Maggie had grown up and lived in my area years ago, I thought she may have been able to share some details about the Patch Lane farm. Any background information could have helped us figure out who our mystery woman was.

"Did you know Joseph Muller?" I asked.

"Yes, I did. Well, sort of. I never met him, but he used to call the insurance company where I worked all the time to report property damages to his farm. We handled and processed the claims for his farm insurance provider since they didn't have a local office in the area. They found it was more feasible to sub out all the claim work. He always seemed to have a 'problem' with his property, especially after a storm or renovation project. One time, he called and reported that someone had dug up one of his fields and he 'lost' a $10,000 crop of corn." Aunt Maggie used air quotes to magnify certain words in her story. She continued, "We didn't even handle crop damage claims, but he wouldn't stop calling. He claimed he had property damage as well, so the firm sent a field technician to investigate. Turned out he had dug up the field himself and had accidentally hit an unmarked utility line that sparked and partially burned the field. He was extremely lucky that the utility company didn't press charges or sue him for the repair costs. We had a tough supervisor at the time, and he finally intervened and convinced the insurance company to terminate his coverage based on the fraudulent claim."

"Wow, he really did try tricks of all kinds."

"Oh yes, he did. He even tried to get one girl at the insurance firm to reinstate his coverage without a supervisor's authorization. She denied having any connections to him, but she was still fired when they discovered the policy change. You don't risk your career for a random client. I suspect she was dating Joseph."

Aunt Maggie had piqued my interest. It was amazing to me that she knew all of this. "Do you remember her name?"

"Yes, I do. Her name was Betty Ann, but everyone called her Beat. I think her married name was Smith or Smooth or something like that. I'm not sure if she changed it after her divorce. I lost track of her after she left the company."

How ironic. Chief Fox's secretary had the same name. I couldn't help but laugh.

"What's so funny?" Aunt Maggie asked.

"Well, Chief Fox's secretary is named Betty Ann and sometimes he'll call her Beat Box. We always laugh about it since we didn't think that Chief Fox knew what a beat box was."

"Oh, wait a minute. I'll bet your Beat Box is the same one I worked with all those years ago. There can't be too many women in town called Beat. If it's the same person, she'd be close to my age or maybe a few years older than I am. I haven't seen her in years, but she used to have the prettiest chestnut brown hair. She always wore it in an old updo style with a black ribbon tied around it. She thought she looked like a movie starlet but if you asked me, she looked more like a cartoon character."

I couldn't believe it! The chief's secretary had the same hairstyle. It had to be the same person. I pulled out my phone and began to scroll through my photos from our last department holiday party. I knew I had a photo of her and I wanted to see if Aunt Maggie recognized her. I found one and enlarged the portion with Betty Ann.

"Does this look like her?" I asked eagerly.

Aunt Maggie studied the photo and said, "Yes, that's her. She's gained a lot of weight and you can tell she colors her hair, but that looks like her."

I began to wonder my questions out loud, "How could Chief Fox not have known this? Why would he hire her then?"

Aunt Maggie actually responded to my rhetorical questions. "Well I can't say for certain, but I wouldn't be surprised if Beat was forced to sign a confidentiality agreement keeping her from disclosing her termination. Plus, it was much easier back then to simply leave things off of your resume. Nowadays you can't get away with that because of all the technology and ways to check."

My mind began to race. Could Betty Ann be the mole in the department? Was the chief aware or, heaven forbid, could he be a *part* of the leak? From what I knew, Chief was a straight shooter. Granted, a sexist one, but nonetheless, he was a fervent supporter of the justice system, so I really didn't think he could be involved. Still, I had to be sure. People's lives were at risk. I glanced down at my watch and saw it was almost 2200 hours. I decided to wait until morning to call Matt and tell him about Aunt Maggie's information on Betty Ann.

We stayed outside just long enough to see a single lightning bolt in the distance. Aunt Maggie and I then moved inside and reclined on the sofa. She always watched the ten o'clock nightly news so I knew she wouldn't want to miss it. I didn't want to worry her about Betty Ann, so I changed the conversation to a lighter topic, Hallie. That wonderful little purr monster had won my aunt's heart and seemed totally at home nestled on her wingback chair.

"What do you think of my newest family addition?" I asked.

"Your little friend is an angel. I'm so glad you have her to keep you company." Aunt Maggie gave Hallie a few strokes as she responded.

"She is. I never knew I could love her as much as I do. I wasn't even looking for a cat, but now I can't imagine life without her."

I glanced at the mantle clock and saw it was almost time for the nightly news. I refilled our wine glasses and grabbed some popcorn from the kitchen. Aunt Maggie loved popcorn, so I knew she would enjoy sharing a bowl with me.

I settled on the couch and covered my legs with a throw. I didn't even have to call Hallie. She leapt from the back of the chair and landed squarely on my lap. I swear this cat had a blanket radar. Aunt Maggie laughed and commented on Hallie's agility. Clearly her paw felt much better and was healing.

The news began promptly at 2200 hours and the first story was no shocker—more rain in the forecast. Aunt Maggie was the first to comment. "I swear, if it rains much more, I'll have to build an ark!"

"So much for April showers bring May flowers. More like April showers bring more May showers."

I complained about how busy Amber Forest Police became when it rained this heavily for days. I expected to be inundated with calls for flooded basements, trapped elderly, and stupid motorists who believed their vehicles could double as boats when the water rose too high for driving. Seriously, we could have gotten new gear and additional officers with the amount of money the department spent rescuing those people last year alone.

The next stories talked about the weather disruption to the local baseball league game schedule. Apparently, the league supervisors were discussing a shortened season and wanted public feedback at the next meeting. Amber Forest really needed to raise the bar on what was considered newsworthy. Aunt Maggie and I laughed at the dramatization by the reporters. We ended up staying awake and watching one of our favorite romantic comedies, eventually calling it a night around 0200 hours.

Chapter 30

I woke to the smell of freshly cooked bacon and coffee. I walked into the kitchen and found a grand breakfast waiting for me while Aunt Maggie was finishing the dishes.

"This looks amazing! It smells just as good, too. Can I help you with the dishes?"

"Oh no, honey. I'm just about finished. I'll join you in a minute!"

I poured myself a cup of coffee. *Mmm.* I could smell the subtle scent of chocolate and cinnamon. My dad had learned his coffee recipe from Aunt Maggie. I made myself a plate of bacon, eggs, toast, and a cinnamon roll. By the time I'd sat down, Aunt Maggie was making her own plate.

"I haven't had a breakfast this good since...well, since the last time I was here! Thank you so much." I was glad I was still in my elastic-waisted pajama pants, so I didn't have to unbutton them as my stomach expanded.

I cleaned up my dishes and headed back to my room to pack up my things. Hallie watched me from her perch on the corner of the desk. Now that I had a full stomach and caffeine in me, I sat down to call Matt.

Matt answered after the second ring. "Hey, Sarah, I was just about to call you."

"Oh, really? What's up?" I let Matt share his information first.

"Listen. I got word that Joseph posted bail."

What the hell? That bastard was supposed to be remanded until trial based on flight risk! *Who posted the bail and what was that judge thinking?* I asked out loud, "How in the hell did that happen?"

"Apparently his lawyer argued that he has advanced prostate cancer and requires pain management and chemotherapy treatment that cannot be provided in the jail. The judge bought the argument and set bail at one million dollars. I guess no one thought he would be able to post it, but within thirty minutes, he was walking out the door."

"Who posted the bail?"

"Well, that's another problem. The paperwork is missing and the camera above the bail office wasn't functioning. We have no visual of who posted that bail. If you ask me, it looks like Muller had some help. Needless to say, this is a real shitstorm. Sarah, I think there's a mole in your department and I'm worried about you."

"I can handle myself. I think you're right though. I think there's a goddamn mole." I was formulating how I wanted to explain Betty Ann to Matt when he interrupted my thoughts.

"We're looking for Muller now, but there's no telling where he's gone. I don't want to alarm you, but I'm worried he could try to come after you. He has a score to settle with you. I'm going to post up two Marshals at your location. I'm on my way back from Pittsburgh as we speak. Are you home right now?"

"No, I'm actually in Hedgewood Township at my aunt's house. Can you come here? I think my aunt has some information you're going to want to hear." Since he was already on his way back from Pittsburgh, I thought it would be even better if Aunt Maggie told him herself.

"Alright. Text me the address and I'll be there in about an hour."

I did as he asked and, true to his word, he and a few of his cavalry arrived within the hour.

Matt came to the front door and Aunt Maggie let him inside. "Hi. I'm Maggie, Sarah's aunt." Stress lines had appeared on her brow and she was wringing her hands. She was clearly worried about me.

"Hello, ma'am. I'm Deputy Sloan with the U.S. Marshals. Feel free to call me Matt. Is Sarah here?" As I walked around the corner, Matt redirected his conversation to me, getting right to business. "Where is a good place for us all to sit down and talk?" He glanced back at Aunt Maggie. "I've been told you have some information I might like to hear?"

"We can talk here in the living room," I answered. "Aunt Maggie, do you think you could throw a pot of coffee on?"

"Absolutely! I'm ready for another cup myself."

Aunt Maggie headed towards the kitchen as I walked Matt to the living room. I teased him, trying to lighten the mood, "Don't worry. She has fresh cream and sugar you can add to your coffee. She might even have a pacifier lying around here from when I was little, too, if you need that."

Matt laughed, "I'm never going to live that down, am I?"

"Oh, absolutely not."

When the coffee was ready, Aunt Maggie returned, and told us that we could help ourselves. We each poured a cup and returned to the living room.

"My, you certainly brought backup," Aunt Maggie commented as she glanced out her front window at the three unmarked police vehicles sitting in the rain.

"Oh yeah, don't mind them," Matt answered. "My guys are out there to keep watch."

Aunt Maggie repeated her story of Betty Ann's prior work experience and subsequent dismissal from the insurance firm. Matt hurriedly took notes, attempting to write as quickly as she spoke. He asked her questions, some that she could answer, others she couldn't. When she finished, she offered to leave the room and headed to the kitchen to give us some privacy.

Matt looked at me seriously and explained, "We're worried Joseph is going to come after you. You're the one who caught him, and he's shown signs of aggression towards all law enforcement throughout this entire process. Even though his cancer is in an advanced phase, that guy is still kicking hard. Not to mention, he probably still has easy access to weapons through his connections. We want to keep a few of our guys with you in case he tries to come after you."

Great. I needed babysitters again. "You guys really don't have to stay with me. I can handle myself."

Matt made it clear that this was not up for discussion. There were going to be suits following me indefinitely until we caught Joseph. I accepted that this decision was out of my hands, and I returned to my room to finish packing up my things.

Aunt Maggie stopped me, and I could hear the nerves in her voice when she asked, "Honey, you don't have to leave now, do you?"

"I really should. I don't want to put you in any danger in case Joseph is able to track me here. Plus, I need to get back to work today. As much as I would love to stay here, I really can't."

"Oh, alright. How about dinner on your next night off?" Aunt Maggie bargained with me.

"If you twist my arm, alright." I gave Aunt Maggie a hug and thanked her for her hospitality. I was surprised to see that Matt did the exact same thing. I wouldn't have been surprised if he'd called her Aunt Maggie as well.

I walked Matt to the front porch, and he stared out into the weather and said, "Man, I can't believe how hard this rain is coming down." He turned towards me and added, "Just give me the signal when you're ready to go and I'll follow you home."

"Aren't you going to try to interview Betty Ann now? I can make it to my apartment safely."

"We can't bring her in for questioning without having solid evidence. We have to make sure we know our shit. I believe everything your Aunt Maggie told me, but I need to have my guys do a little digging and get some concrete evidence to back up our line of questioning before we try to get her to talk."

I didn't like waiting, but I knew Matt was right. I finished packing and had to make five trips out to my car to load my suitcase, Hallie's litter box, her bed, and my shopping bag full of items for her. Aunt Maggie saw that both me and my belongings were getting soaked.

"Sarah, don't you have a bag for Hallie's items?"

"Yeah, I just put it in the car," I told her.

"No, I mean a real bag. Not a shopping bag."

"Oh, um, I guess not. I didn't have a bag the right size."

"Wait right here." Aunt Maggie ran upstairs and came back down with a designer brand cloth travel bag, made for a day trip. "Here you go! This can be Hallie's bag."

I couldn't help but laugh at the fact that Hallie was about to have her own designer bag worth more than my off-brand suitcase. "Thank you, Aunt Maggie, I'm sure Hallie will appreciate it!"

I gave Aunt Maggie another big hug and thanked her for everything before I carried Hallie out to my car and started my trip home. Matt and one of the other unmarked cars followed me back to my apartment. I suspected that the other vehicles had plans to follow up on some of Aunt Maggie's information. I took the shade way home, driving slow through the rain. The creeks were rising, and I prayed they didn't flood. I knew work would be chaos if we had another episode of flooding.

I didn't want to get Hallie wet, so after I parked my car, I ran up to my apartment to open the door before carrying her inside. It was still rainy and dreary, so my apartment was almost completely dark. I reached over to flip on the light switch, screaming as soon as the lights turned on. There was a man standing next to my fireplace, holding a gun. It was Joseph.

"You goddamn pig. I'm gonna shut you up once and for all," Joseph said as he slowly raised his gun.

"Why are you here? Why do you want me dead? I'm not the one after you—the feds are! I'm just a small-town cop!" My words sounded distant as I pleaded for my life. I could feel my gun in my waistband under my shirt, but I knew that if I reached for it, he would pull the trigger faster than I could get it out.

"You're the one who found the body. You're the reason I had to leave my farm. You know, at first, I thought it was a strange coincidence, but then I came to learn that your dad, Officer Hastings, was the one who helped my tenant snitch on me twenty years ago. I'm gonna kill you, and then I'll kill your dad next."

Joseph put his finger on the trigger, and I heard three rapid gunshots. I stood in my doorway, frozen, watching as Joseph collapsed to the floor. I looked down to check myself for a wound. As I did, I saw someone out of the corner of my eye rush into my apartment from behind me. It was Matt.

Matt radioed for backup, keeping his gun out as he approached Joseph. When he was sure it was safe to do so, Matt holstered his weapon and handcuffed Joseph. I was still standing in my doorway, shocked that I didn't have a bullet hole through my torso. Eventually the second deputy, then the third, entered and rendered assistance. It felt like only seconds before everyone else arrived on scene, although I'm sure it was at minimum several minutes. It's funny how sometimes five seconds can feel like ten minutes, and at other times ten minutes can feel like five seconds. I was sure the shock was playing tricks on my concept of time.

Once my apartment was flooded with uniforms and Joseph was dragged away on a gurney, Matt sat down on my couch with me. "Sarah. You're alright. It's okay. I'm sorry. We had no idea Joseph snuck into your apartment. I had a guy posted out front, but he must have snuck in through a window or through the back."

"What the hell happened? I'm fine, but I'll be honest, I'm a little in shock. That goddamn asshole." I was visibly shaking but tried to put on a brave face.

"I would be shaken too, if someone broke into my home. You have every right to be in shock." Matt tried his best to comfort me.

"Where is he now?"

"He was transported to the hospital...but I got word that he's dead. He's going to be taken to the Medical Examiner's."

I looked over to my fireplace and saw the massive pool of blood on my carpet. Matt caught me staring and offered, "I can find you a good cleanup crew. We're going to be processing this scene for a while. I think this goes without saying, but you'll need to stay somewhere else tonight."

I thought about where I could go. Poor Hallie was still in my car and I knew I needed to go let her out somewhere. I considered going back to Aunt Maggie's, but I also really wanted to go see my dad.

"Yeah, I'm gonna go to my dad's. Did any of your guys look into Betty Ann yet?" I knew it had only been an hour or two since we'd left Aunt Maggie's, but I was nervous and wanted that bitch caught. She could have been the one who killed Michelle.

"My guys are still looking into her. They already found enough that they think we should pick her up at the station before she's done with work. I promise I'm going to take care of it." Matt went to speak with one of the other suits in my apartment. He came back and told me, "Alright, they have everything handled here, so I'm going to head to the station to question Betty Ann myself."

"I need to let Hallie out of her crate, so I should head to my dad's right now. But if you're going to go question Betty Ann, then I sure as hell want to be there for that. I have no doubt in my mind she's our mole and I want to take her down." I didn't realize how loudly I was speaking until I saw some of the other deputies turn around and stare at me.

Matt was surprised by my intrepidness, but agreed to let me observe while he interviewed Betty Ann. He followed me to my dad's, where I ran Hallie and all her belongings inside. I explained everything as quickly as I could to my dad, and he was happy to help me by watching Hallie. For someone who was a dog person, he was awfully relieved that Hallie was alright. I warned him about Betty Ann and Joseph's threat on his life. Before I'd finished my sentence, my dad had reached under his couch and pulled out a loaded shotgun.

"Jesus Christ, Dad, has that been there this entire time?!"

"Ah, only since I retired, and I knew no children would be crawling around here." He looked pleased with himself as he held up his shotgun.

"Alright, Dad. I guess I should worry about Betty Ann more than I should worry about you, huh?" I gave him a big bear hug and ran back out the door. I decided to leave my car at my dad's, riding with Matt instead. I was still recovering from shock, so I was glad I didn't have to get behind the wheel just yet. However, when we were only a block away from the station, Matt turned off into Dina's coffeeshop.

"Uh, did you want to grab coffee before grabbing Betty Ann?" I was confused by the detour.

Matt shut off the car and turned towards me. "My guys are going to meet us here with everything they found on Betty Ann. We need a game plan before we go bursting in and grabbing her. It's only 1500 hours now, so she should be at the station for another hour or two. We have plenty of time to do this right."

"Oh, that makes more sense than an unexpected coffee craving," I responded.

A few minutes later, one of the unmarked cruisers positioned alongside Matt's vehicle so that the driver's windows were next to each other.

I recognized the deputy in the other car as Matt's partner, but I couldn't recall his name. I was glad when he said, "Hi, Officer Hastings. It's been a while. I'm Deputy Jackson."

"Oh! Hello Deputy. How's your wife and new baby doing?" I hadn't seen Deputy Jackson since the first time I met Matt. I guess he came back into town when Joseph made bail and was on the run.

"We're all doing very well, thank you for asking." Deputy Jackson handed a folder to Matt. "Bet you guys can't guess what we found on your Betty Ann."

"You're right. I'm never going to guess it, so why don't you get on with it and tell me?" Matt teased Deputy Jackson.

"Alright, alright. For starters, her official name is Betty Ann Whittle."

"Yes, that's what I know her as," I chimed in.

Deputy Jackson continued, "Right. But that isn't her birth name. She was born as Betty Ann Salto. She got married when she was only eighteen years old and changed her last name to Smoothe. She ended up getting divorced and eventually picked the last name Whittle. We found no other connection to this last name, so she probably just picked a random new one. That isn't where it gets good, though. While we were looking into her childhood name changes, we also looked into her family members. Betty Ann was a foster child. Guess where she lived for a good portion of her childhood?"

"Oh my god, don't tell me she lived at Patch Lane," I blurted out.

"No. But I can respect that guess." Jackson went on, "She lived on Fiddle Lane with the Lucketts. I'll bet you any money she knew about that house being empty and told Joseph he would be safe to hide out there."

Wow, I was impressed with Jackson's investigation skills. I understood why Matt liked him as a partner so much. Matt said, "This is all great. You find anything else?"

"Well, not surprisingly, it turns out Hastings' aunt was spot on. We confirmed Betty Ann's prior employment and looked into the allegations. Given all of this, we were able to obtain a search warrant. We have a team about to hit her house while we go pick her up at the station for questioning."

Matt flipped through the papers that Jackson handed him and looked up. "Damn, you work fast, man. This is awesome. You guys ready?"

We gave Matt the signal and all of us headed down the block to the station. We went in through the rear entrance and headed towards Betty Ann's desk. When we finally reached her desk, it was empty, and the computer screen was black. I followed Matt upstairs and asked Chief Fox if he knew where Betty Ann had gone.

"Beat got sick and went home," Chief Fox told Matt.

"How long ago was that?" Matt asked.

"She left only a short while after the shooting. I told her not to worry about it, since the entire station has been empty, with everyone rushing to the scene."

We ran back downstairs, and as we passed by Betty Ann's desk I heard, "Dispatch to 1050." There was a police radio sitting right on the corner of her desk. She must have heard when Joseph was shot. *Shit.*

Chapter 31

Matt requested that Amber Forest issue an APB on Betty Ann and we started strategizing where to send our guys. We directed some uniformed cops to her house to assist the suits with their search warrant. We also contacted the tech nerds and had them look into whether or not we could ping her cellphone and vehicle. I kept running through different scenarios and places in my head where Betty Ann could have fled. There was no way she would return to Patch Lane or Fiddle Lane knowing that the cops had already put those places on our radar.

"I think I know where she went! Well, kind of," I blurted out to Matt.

"Let's hear it," Matt egged me to keep talking.

"She doesn't know we're on to her yet. She left here because she heard Joseph was shot. She either ran to the hospital to try to see him or the Medical Examiner's to try to see his body, or something along those lines. Regardless, I bet she left to be with Joseph."

"You're right. There's no way she would have known we were on to her before she left the station." Matt grabbed his car keys, and as he was walking towards the rear of the building he yelled back, "Well, aren't you coming?"

I jumped into Matt's car and we raced to the hospital. We hurried into the ER and ran up to the nearest nurses' station. There were a few men and women in scrubs doing various jobs behind the desk.

Matt quickly asked, "Have any of you seen a woman come in here looking for a Joseph Muller?"

The nurses exchanged silent glances, and eventually one of them spoke up, "No, I haven't. I don't think anyone else has either."

Damnit.

I recognized one of the nurses. I'd built a good relationship with her because of all the suicidal patients I'd brought in as a CIT officer. I saw her off to the side, hunched over a portable computer station. I nudged Matt and we headed towards her. "Hey Lisa, can I snag you for a minute?"

Lisa looked up at me with bright, eager eyes. "Sure, Sarah!" We stepped inside an empty patient room. She asked curiously, "What's up?"

"You can't tell anyone about this conversation, okay?" I didn't want there to be a commotion at the hospital.

"Absolutely. You have my word."

Matt looked at me with such a hard stare that I could already hear him yelling *Don't you dare tell her confidential information!*

I continued, "We are currently looking for a person of interest. We think she might have tried to come here because she thought someone she loved was rushed here. If she wanted to sneak in unnoticed and look for someone, how do you think she would do that?"

Matt's stare lessened from a yell to more of an *Ugh* look, relieved I didn't give away confidential information, but still not happy I gave away some information.

Lisa thought for a moment. "Hmm. We actually had something like that happen a couple weeks ago. There was a woman here who was a victim of a domestic assault and her husband snuck into the hospital. One of the nurses found him in her room and had to call security to escort him out. We ended up having to call you guys, but I don't think you were working that night. The balding guy showed up, Peter?"

Peterson. I said, "Oh yeah, I think I heard about that. So, how did the husband sneak in?"

"Oh, right! Sorry. They replayed the surveillance footage and saw that he came in through the hospital's main entrance and waited outside the locked door that leads to the Emergency Room wing. Eventually, one of the employees badged out of the ER and, while the door was open, he snuck in."

"Lisa, this was extremely helpful. Thank you so much!" I gave Matt a proud look as if to say *You should always trust me.*

Matt followed me to the security desk, and I saw Rusty was working that night. "Hey Rusty, how's it going?"

"Aww, well look at that, if it isn't Officer Hastings. Long time no see, I thought there were no more suicidal people left in this town for a minute," Rusty joked. When you constantly work around dying people and criminals, your sense of humor tends to turn dark.

Matt introduced himself and shook Rusty's hand.

"How's the application going with the police academy?" I wanted to soften the conversation before asking Rusty for a favor.

"Oh, you know how it is. It's a slow process. I applied and just recently got scheduled to take the PT test in two weeks. I've been running every other day and working on my sit-ups."

"Good for you, I have no doubt you'll pass! Let me know if I can help you with anything."

"Thanks, Sarah, I appreciate that! What brings you and Deputy Sloan in tonight?"

"I can't really say, but I was hoping you could do us a huge favor and review some security footage." I flashed a smile at Rusty.

"Of course! I'm happy to help."

That was one thing I always liked about Rusty. He wanted to become a cop so badly that he would do anything and everything he could to help us out when we asked him. I told him the time frame to pull footage from and asked him to play it at ten times the speed.

We sat and watched the video footage from the main hospital doors near the emergency wing and after only three minutes I jumped off my stool and yelled, "THERE!"

Rusty stopped the video and rewound the footage. He instinctually picked up that we were looking at the older woman who had entered the ER. "Oh damn, how did I miss that?" Rusty was kicking himself for not seeing that this stranger had passed through a non-public access.

"It's alright, Rusty. Can you try to follow this woman through the video footage, though, and see where she went?" I asked.

Rusty was quick with his fingers and easily pulled up all the footage we needed. We watched Betty Ann walk through the ER, checking all the rooms, and eventually make her way out through the exit. Rusty was a step ahead of us and pulled up the surveillance footage of her walking through the parking lot and to her car.

"That's her car. I always thought it was the ugliest shade of purple," I said to Matt as we watched her climb into her car.

I glanced to the bottom right corner of the screen to check the timestamp. She'd gotten into her car at 1137 hours. I looked at my watch and saw it was 1150 hours. She'd left the hospital thirteen minutes ago.

"Damnit. We just missed her," I said aloud.

"Alright. This is helpful. She probably saw the cops swarming her house, so now we have to think where else she would have gone," Matt verbalized his thought process.

We began to leave, and I asked Rusty to burn a copy of the video footage and send it to me. I added, "By the way, this is still under investigation so don't mention anything we reviewed to anyone. Cool?"

"Oh, definitely. I won't say a word," Rusty assured me. I believed him too, since he had always respected my requests in the past.

Matt and I left and began to brainstorm Betty Ann's next step. While we were sitting in the parking lot thinking, Matt got a phone call.

"Sloan, go ahead." Then he replied, "Awesome. Give me the address so I can write it down." He scribbled an address on his notepad, then responded, "Okay, got it. Keep me posted with live updates if her location changes." He hung up the phone.

"What was that?" I asked.

"My guys were able to get a search warrant for Betty Ann's cellphone and got her location. She's still in Amber Forest. Put your seatbelt on." Matt passed me the address that he'd scribbled on the piece of paper and asked, "Can you tell me how to get there?"

I looked down at the address. "Yeah. That's my dad's house."

Patch Lane

Barkley

Chapter 32

Matt flipped on his lights and siren and I jumped on my radio. "1034 to all units. Any and all available units respond to 5367 Juliet Drive. Our suspect is at that location, which is Officer Stuart Hastings' home. Respond immediately."

Everyone jumped on the radio to show that they were en route to my dad's house. My dad lived only five minutes from the hospital, so with the way Matt was driving we arrived in under three minutes. I tried to jump out of the car, forgetting that I still had my seatbelt buckled. I fumbled to unlatch it and ran to catch up with Matt. I threw open my dad's front door and yelled, "DAD!" My heart was racing, and adrenaline was pumping through my veins. *If anything happens to my dad, I will personally take care of Betty Ann.*

I heard the sirens of all the other cruisers pulling up to our location. I ran through the family room and into the dining room, where I found my dad on the ground with a pool of blood around him. "Oh my God! Dad!"

My dad was still alive and had tied his belt around his leg as a makeshift tourniquet. He quickly responded, "That bitch just shot me. She ran out back! I'm fine, GO!"

I refused to leave my dad, so Matt raced out the back door and I got on the radio. "1034 to all units. Suspect shot one victim and ran out the back door of the residence. Deputy Sloan is pursuing the suspect and backup is needed. I'm rendering aid to the victim inside the residence.

Adult male, alert and conscious, gunshot wound to his leg. Tourniquet applied. Send me an ambulance."

I turned back to my dad and ripped my emergency first aid kit off my duty belt. I applied gauze to his wound and pressure on his thigh. I made him lie down while I slid my legs under his leg, propping it up to reduce the flow of blood. "Dad, what happened?"

"It was Beat! That secretary! She came through the front door and shot me. Thank God she had terrible aim, hah. I was sitting here in the dining room and she shot me from the front door. She heard the sirens coming and ran out the back."

"You're going to be alright. We have an ambulance on the way." I continued to apply pressure to my dad's wound. I could tell he was in pain, but he was so goddamn strong.

"Bitch is lucky I wasn't in the family room, or else she'd have buckshot in her skull right now." My dad's anger was keeping him awake, so I let him continue his rant. "She was always a bitch to work with. Sarah, I'm really fine. You can go."

"No. I'm not leaving you."

My radio clicked on. "1045 to Dispatch. I'm with Marshal Sloan and we have one in custody."

"Dad, did you hear that? Tim is with Matt and they have her. They have Betty Ann." I did my best to keep my dad talking, but he was losing a lot of blood. He became quieter and was slowly closing his eyes.

My radio clicked on again. "Dispatch to 1034."

"1034, go," I quickly responded.

"Paramedics are on scene but want to make sure the scene is safe to enter."

"Yes, the scene is safe. Have them enter immediately."

The paramedics came through the front door and rushed to render aid to my dad, doing a much better job than I had. I followed them to the ambulance, wanting to ride in the back with my dad, but I knew I was needed at the scene. I held his hand and promised that I would meet him at the hospital soon. I gave the paramedics Aunt Maggie's phone number and asked as a personal favor that they call her to tell her where they would be taking my dad. They agreed without hesitation and I ran back to my dad's house. Since Hallie was still there somewhere, I ran inside and closed all the doors. I began to look for her in a hurry, and sure enough, I found her in my dad's bedroom, curled up under his bed, terrified. I closed the bedroom door and quickly taped a note to it that read:

Do Not Open

-Officer Sarah Hastings

I ran back downstairs and saw Matt loading Betty Ann into the back of Tim's marked cruiser. I walked up to them and asked, "Are you guys taking her back to the station for questioning?"

Matt and Tim both looked surprised and Tim asked, "Sarah, why aren't you with your dad? I thought you would have gone to the hospital with him."

"He's going to be alright. He's tough. I wanted to finish this, once and for all." I had hate in my eyes as I looked at Betty Ann in the backseat of Tim's cruiser.

I followed Matt and Tim to the station, walking a safe distance behind them as they took Betty Ann into the interrogation room. I worried that if I was too close to her, I would do something irrational. They cuffed her wrists to the table and secured her ankles to the chain on the floor. Matt and Tim stood in the hallway plotting their questioning strategy.

"I can't wait to get in there and tear her apart," I said in a voice so hostile that even I didn't recognize it as mine.

Matt looked at me for a moment before he spoke. "Sarah…you can't go in there."

"What the hell do you mean I can't go in there? She shot my dad!"

"That's exactly why you can't go in there! You're too close to this. You know that. Don't make this any harder on yourself."

I hated when Matt told me what was good for me. I hated it even more when he was right. "Ugh. Alright, fine. But I'm going to go watch from the video surveillance room."

"I think that's a great idea. We'll consult with you on breaks," Matt said, as if it was my bright idea rather than him pushing me into this position.

I made my way into the video surveillance room and situated myself in the wooden chair. I watched the screen as Matt walked into the interrogation room, followed by Tim. Matt took a seat across the table from Betty Ann while Tim stood in the corner against the wall, as if he was Matt's bodyguard.

Matt took out a card from his credential wallet and read, "I'm Deputy U.S. Marshal Sloan. I am accompanied by Officer Briggs today to interview Ms. Betty Ann Whittle." Matt read the date, time, and Miranda Rights aloud for the record. Afterward he asked, "Ms. Whittle, do you understand your rights as I have read them to you?"

"Yeah," Betty Ann responded.

"Are you currently under the influence of any drugs, alcohol, or anything else that could impair your responses to our questions?"

"Do I look high to you? No." Betty Ann crossed her arms as she sat back in her chair.

"And what is your highest level of education?" Matt asked.

"What the hell does that matter? You think I'm too stupid to understand my rights?"

"No, ma'am. It's standard protocol that I ask you what your highest level of education is to establish that you are competent to comprehend your rights," Matt explained.

"High school."

"I'm going to ask you a few basic questions about your background. When's your birthday?" Matt asked.

Betty Ann sat upright. "Now, didn't your mother ever tell you that it was rude to ask a lady her age?"

Matt gave a half-assed smile as he replied, "Ms. Whittle, can you please just respond to my question?"

"No." Betty Ann was not cooperating.

"Alright, I'll move on. We found that you were born Ms. Betty Ann Salto, but got married in 1981 and changed your name to Mrs. Betty Ann Smoothe. After your divorce, you decided to use the name Whittle. Is that correct?" Matt asked.

Betty Ann coldly stared at Matt. She pursed her lips, emphasizing the wrinkles around her mouth. She refused to answer. She wasn't going to make this easy.

I felt my phone buzz. It was Aunt Maggie. She'd texted me to tell me that my dad was doing well and they were taking him into surgery. She ended her text telling me that she would keep me updated. I wished I could have been in two places at once, but I knew Aunt Maggie would take care of my dad and I knew he would understand why I had to be here.

I redirected my focus back to the monitor. I had no idea how, but Matt looked calm and cool. I wasn't even in the interrogation room, but I was so heated I could feel the steam coming off my forehead. I guess it really was a good call that I'd stayed behind the curtain.

Matt decided to step things up a bit. "You want to tell us why you shot Stuart Hastings today? We all know you shot him, we were on scene and saw you run out the back. You still had the gun on you."

Betty Ann scooted to the edge of her seat. She placed both of her elbows on the table and slowly leaned over, grinning as she responded, "You know what I want?"

"What's that?" Matt asked, still sitting straight in his chair, unfazed by Betty Ann's tactics.

"I want my goddamn lawyer."

Shit.

"If that's how you want to play this, then be my guest. I'll go arrange for you to call your lawyer. I'll be right back," Matt coolly replied.

How the hell was he staying so calm? Matt and Tim left the interview room and walked down the short hallway to the surveillance room I was sitting in. As soon as Matt was far enough away from the interview room, he yelled, "DAMNIT!"

"Whoa there." I was shocked at Matt's mini blow up. He seemed like he barely cared this entire time.

"That bitch is lawyering up," Matt said as he was huffing and puffing.

"Yeah, I saw," I said confusedly. "You, uh, you really put on quite the act in there. I really thought you were that detached."

Matt slowed his breathing and responded, "Well I guess that means I'm doing my job pretty damn well."

I was taken aback by Matt's forwardness. He was usually much softer. Meanwhile, Tim had had a pissed off look on his face since they'd left my dad's house. Tim was not great at hiding his emotions, but he was good at keeping his mouth shut when he needed to.

Matt turned to Tim. "Briggs, do you mind taking Betty Ann to the phone so that she can call her lawyer? I'm going to touch base with my guys serving the search warrant on her place."

Tim answered, "Yeah, you got it boss," and headed back to the interview room to escort Betty Ann to the phone.

Matt took his cellphone out of his back pocket and leaned his butt against the counter in the surveillance room. The room was only about eight feet long by eight feet wide, so there was barely enough room for the two of us.

Matt dialed his phone and held it up to his ear. "Hey, what do you have going on over there?" Matt stayed on the phone for nearly ten minutes.

I tried to make out what was being said on the phone, but I couldn't tell what the person on the other end was saying. Finally, Matt got off the phone and I asked, "Well...?"

"My guys are awesome. You wouldn't believe what they found so far," Matt excitedly said. "It was good we had the element of surprise on our side and she didn't see us coming. They were going through her computer files and found she had created a fundraising website to raise money for Michelle's son, Ryan. It was in her browser history and she was still logged into the website. That has to be what brought Michelle out of hiding! Betty Ann knew if she posted enough things online about Ryan dying, Michelle would find it. Michelle came out of hiding because she thought her son had cancer. Damn."

"But how did Betty Ann know that Michelle was in hiding and wasn't really dead?" I asked.

"That's something we'll have to ask her once her lawyer gets here."

"Do you think you have enough to charge her?" I asked.

"Well, we definitely have enough to charge her with several crimes, but I'm not convinced we have enough to pin her for Michelle's murder. We really only have circumstantial evidence tying her to it. I told my guys to call me with more updates as they continue their search. They're great at what they do. Now I need to hold up my end. I need to break her."

We were in the surveillance room for about twenty minutes discussing all the newly found information when Betty Ann's lawyer arrived at the station. The man was balding, had thick rimmed glasses, and walked with a slight hunch. I wasn't too impressed with the guy until Tim said, "Ah, shit. She got Robert Munsin. That guy's one of the sharpest lawyers in Amber Forest."

"Really?" I asked. "He doesn't look like one of the top-notch lawyers."

"I know he doesn't quite look the part, but he's a complete book nerd. He knows every single law; he knows his shit. Almost all of his objections are sustained in court and he knows how to prep his witnesses." Tim looked concerned.

Matt joined our conversation and replied, "I'm not worried about this guy. I'm still gonna ask my same questions, and if she has half a brain, she'll cooperate. I'll make sure of that."

Tim directed Mr. Munsin to the interview room and allowed him to become acquainted with his newest client, Betty Ann. After several minutes, Matt and Tim entered the interview room to continue their line of questioning.

Matt stated the date and time for the record and asked Mr. Munsin to formally introduce himself. Once the record was clear, Matt continued with his line of questioning. "Alright, Ms. Whittle. As I was asking you earlier, would you like to explain to us why you shot Stuart Hastings earlier today?"

Mr. Munsin interrupted and said to Betty Ann, "You don't have to answer that."

Betty Ann grinned as she slyly remarked, "See, I guess it was a good thing I got my lawyer. I don't have to answer that."

"What has Officer Hastings or his daughter ever done to you? Why do you hate them?"

Mr. Munsin began to tell Betty Ann, "You don't—"

Betty Ann interrupted him and answered Matt's question anyway. "Those pigs stick their snouts where they don't belong. The bitch should have listened to my warning."

Mr. Munsin threw his body back into his chair, dropped his pen on the table, and rolled his eyes into the back of his head. He was not happy with his client.

Her warning? How had she warned me? I remembered the pig's head at my door. This entire time, I'd made the mistake of assuming it was mafia-related and hadn't even considered it could have been Betty Ann.

Matt could tell he was slowly creeping into Betty Ann's head. He proceeded with his questioning. "How did you warn her?"

Mr. Munsin was faster and louder to interrupt this time. "Don't answer that!"

Betty Ann wore anger across her face, but she listened to her lawyer and didn't say a word.

"Listen, you're going to be locked up for a long time. We have you for shooting Officer Stuart Hastings. You don't love Joseph. You know how I know that? Because you're willing to sit here and be uncooperative rather than give him a proper burial. We know he has no family and no one to attend a funeral besides you. If you cooperate, we can make sure that you're able to attend his funeral. However, if you keep this act up, then he's going to be thrown into the ground with the dirt kicked over him. Right now, it's entirely up to you how Joseph is going to be remembered and memorialized. So, what's it going to be? Do you love him or not?"

Mr. Munsin leaned over to whisper something to Betty Ann, but before he could even get a word out Betty Ann slammed her fists on the table. "How dare you accuse me of not loving Joseph! I did everything for that man! I sacrificed my entire life for him! Everything I did, I did for Joseph's dying wish. He knew in his gut Michelle was still alive and wanted to make sure she was dead before he was. Then, he wanted those bastard cops killed that helped get him caught in the first place!"

Was that an admission to killing Michelle?

Mr. Munsin covered his face with his right hand as he shook his head. When Betty Ann was finished yelling, he said, "Ms. Whittle. You hired me as your lawyer to protect you not only from the cops but also from yourself. I *highly* suggest you start listening to what I have to say before you respond!"

Matt's tone grew louder. "So what's it going to be, Betty Ann? You going to cooperate and give Joseph a proper burial or let his ashes end up in the trash?"

"What the hell do you want from me?! I killed Michelle, I shot the pig, and you know what? I'd shoot the bitch, too, if I could!" Betty Ann was so far over the table that she was close to falling out of her seat. I'd never seen so much anger and coldness in someone's eyes. Betty Ann was once neat, well-dressed, and wore a perfect bun with a single black ribbon in her hair. As I stared at her on the monitor, I saw a crazed, disheveled woman who had snapped. Her hair was no longer neat, but a tangled mess instead. Her black ribbon that was once tied so nicely in a bow was now just a knot with two ends of ribbon hanging loose. The woman whose high energy once annoyed me was now a woman I knew would try to kill me with her bare hands if she were given the opportunity.

Matt decided to leave Betty Ann and her lawyer alone to let her cool down. He wanted her to calm down and hopefully realize that cooperating was her best option. Matt and Tim left the interview room and walked back to the surveillance room. "Wow," I said. "You really did break her."

Matt smiled and responded, "That was the goal. I think she's going to come to her senses and cooperate with us now that she's already made all those statements. Her lawyer knows they're screwed, and any lawyer with half a brain, which is probably most lawyers, knows that cooperation is the best option here."

Tim gave Matt a hard pat on the shoulder and said, "You did a pretty damn good job at interviewing for a suit. Nice job in there."

"Please tell me that Betty Ann won't be posting bail when all of this is said and done?" I asked with half sarcasm and half nervousness.

"No. I'm going to make it very clear that she made a threat on your life, and no judge should allow her bail with a threat like that on video," Matt responded.

"Good," I said. "So, how do you think Betty Ann knew to find Michelle at Patch Lane?"

Matt shrugged. "I can't say for certain, but I would guess she had been watching all over Amber Forest waiting to see when and where Michelle would pop up. That online website said that Ryan was at the hospital here in Amber Forest, so she probably got lucky that she first saw Michelle at Patch Lane. Based on what Michelle was wearing and the items in that safe, I suspect she was trying to make sure that Ryan would be able to recognize her when he saw her."

Matt's theory made sense, but I wasn't too sure about how Betty Ann knew Michelle was at Patch Lane. I asked, "Did your guys get Betty Ann's phone calls and text history yet?"

Matt raised his eyebrows and responded, "You know what, I'm not sure. Let me call and ask."

Matt called one of his guys, and before he hung up the phone he asked, "Alright, can you fax them over? Thanks."

"I take that as a good sign?" I asked.

"Yeah. Good thinking. They're faxing the documents to your station now. He warned me it's over a hundred pages."

"Alright. I'll go run over to the fax machine and wait for them. I have an idea."

When the document finally finished printing, I flipped through the pages of text messages to the date of Michelle's murder. I found a conversation between Betty Ann and a phone number that I suspected was Joseph.

The bait worked. Just saw Michelle at the hospital asking about Ryan. I'm going to follow her.

OK.

She's at your farm. Not sure what she's doing here. Will text back soon. Love u.

I showed Matt the conversation. It was all coming together. He excitedly said, "This is fantastic. Good thinking, Sarah. Now you're thinking like a suit." He smirked as he glanced towards Tim. Matt was giving Tim payback for his remark about suits earlier. After he'd had his fun, Matt turned back to me and added, "We're going to get everything we need to lock her up for a long time. Even if she decides not to cooperate, we have enough on her. It's over."

Matt and Tim got ready to head back to the interview room. Tim came up to me and said, "Sarah, we have it from here. You heard Sloan. We already have what we need. Everything from here on out will be icing on the cake. You should go check on your dad. That's where you're needed right now."

"Yeah, you're right. I'll touch base with you guys in a little bit." I gathered my things and saw that one of the older guys from the daylight shift was sitting in the report writing room. A few of them were still on the clock because of the shooting at my apartment earlier. I popped my head in and asked if he could drop me off at my dad's house. To no surprise, he was happy to help.

I stripped off my gear and uniform until I was down to my BDU pants and black undershirt. I switched my gun to my off-duty holster and secured it inside my waistband. Once I was back at my dad's, I got into my car and started towards the hospital.

Chapter 33

"Hey Dad, how ya feeling?" I bent over and gave him a kiss on his forehead as he lay in his hospital bed. I added, "I'm sorry it took me a few hours to get here."

My dad held my hand and responded, "I'm doing alright. They said I should be able to go home within the next couple hours. Luckily the bullet missed all my bones and went straight through. The best nurse here, though, is my favorite sister. Thank you, Maggie."

Aunt Maggie smiled at my dad's compliment and responded, "Oh Stu, of course I'm going to be here at your side. You're my brother."

"So, what's the plan for tonight, Dad? I was thinking I could stay with you, so you're not alone," I suggested.

Aunt Maggie replied, "We actually talked about that already, and I think it would be best if you both stayed at my house for a little while. I have plenty of room and that house gets awfully quiet. Sarah, I know you still have work, so I'm happy to help with your dad while you're on duty."

"That sounds like a perfect plan to me. I just need to go get Hallie from my dad's and swing by the station to finish a few things. I'll meet you both at home tonight?" I asked.

"See you then, sweetie," my dad replied.

I drove to the station first and saw that Matt and Tim were still there finishing up paperwork. "Hey guys," I greeted them.

"Hey, Sarah. How's your dad?" Tim asked.

"He's doing well. He'll be coming home tonight, which is great."

"That's great to hear. You know we have everything from here," Tim assured. "You didn't need to come back for anything."

"Yeah, I know. I stopped by because I didn't get a chance to properly thank you both earlier. You guys stuck with me, even when I dragged your asses into old, creepy tunnels. You never lost faith in me. Anyway, I guess, just thanks." I didn't know how else to explain my appreciation for partners who were so faithful and always had my back, no matter what.

Matt and Tim assured me that I didn't have to thank them for anything because they were happy to work with me.

"Has anyone notified Ryan that we caught his mom's murderer?"

Matt answered, "Not yet. I was going to check if he was still at his great-grandmother's or if he was back in Maryland."

"Do you mind if I handle contacting Ryan?" I never got to tell him about my dad and his mom, and I felt like I owed it to him to tell him the whole story.

"Yeah, I actually think that would be a good idea."

"Thanks. I'll give you a call after I make contact."

I was walking towards the station's rear door when Matt ran after me. He grabbed my arm as I reached to open the door. "Hey Sarah, sorry. I just, uh, wanted to say I really enjoyed getting to know you throughout this case. If you ever find yourself in Pittsburgh, you should give me a call," Matt said, stumbling over his words. "Maybe we could even meet up for a cup of coffee while we're not working sometime? With cream and sugar, of course," he added with a nervous laugh.

I smiled, feeling a rush of warmth to my cheeks as I thanked Matt for the offer.

I left the station in my personal car and decided to stop by Rose's first to see if Ryan was still staying with her. I pulled up to the log cabin and made my way towards Rose's front door, still wearing my BDU's and undershirt. I knocked, and it took Rose a few moments before she recognized me.

"Oh! Sarah! I'm sorry, you look different without your uniform on and it threw me off for a moment. How can I help you?"

"Is Ryan still here by any chance?"

"Yes, he is. He's actually getting his things ready to leave tomorrow morning. Please, come in! Would you like me to start a pot of coffee?"

I normally didn't like to impose on people, but it was getting late and I could feel the weight of the bags under my eyes. "Actually, that would be wonderful. Thank you so much."

I followed Rose inside and sat down at the dining room table while she got Ryan and started the coffee. Ryan came out and greeted me. "Hi, Officer Hastings, it's nice to see you again. Do you have any updates on my mom's murder?"

"Please, call me Sarah. Yes, I actually do. You might want to sit down for this."

Ryan slowly pulled out the wooden chair and sat down. I could smell the coffee brewing in the kitchen.

"We caught the woman who murdered your mom."

Ryan's forehead scrunched and he titled his head. "Woman? Wait, what?"

"It turns out that Joseph Muller wasn't the one who killed your mom. It was actually his girlfriend, Betty Ann. Joseph Muller was diagnosed with stage four prostate cancer and his dying wish was to see your mom dead along with my dad and me. When he wasn't able to carry that out on his own, Betty Ann stepped in to assist. She was the one who made the fake fundraiser for you. She wanted to make it look like you had cancer, to lure your mom out of hiding."

"Wow." Ryan fell back into his chair, and I could tell that he was still processing my words.

Rose came out of the kitchen with a coffee mug and set it on the table in front of me. I thanked her as she joined us. "So, what's the update?" Rose asked.

Ryan answered before I could. "They caught my mom's killer. It was Joseph's girlfriend."

Rose's eyes welled up with tears. "That is certainly good news. Who was she?"

I answered, "Her name is Betty Ann. She's the Amber Forest Police Department's secretary. If you recall, there used to be rumors about a mole in our department. I think it's been her all these years."

Ryan asked, "You said they wanted you and your dad dead, too. But why you guys?"

I took a long sip of my coffee. The hot liquid felt soothing as I swallowed. I inhaled deeply before I divulged the biggest piece of information. "That's actually why I wanted to come here and talk to you personally. Oh boy, where do I start with this one…" I trailed off and took another sip of coffee. "Rose, do you remember when you told me that Michelle was dating a guy right before she went into the Witness Protection Program?"

"Yes, she said he was a very nice man. What about him?"

"She was dating my dad." Before Rose or Ryan could ask me any questions, I jumped into explaining to them how I came to find this out. "I had no idea, I promise. I only recently found out when I was at my dad's and I came across a photograph of Michelle and me. He thought she died twenty years ago like everyone else."

Rose gently held her hand over her mouth as she shook her head. "I can't believe it. What are the chances? Michelle always said such good things about your father… I always wished she would have introduced us."

"Actually, you did meet my dad. Do you remember the story you told me about when Michelle found the young girl's body in the park and an officer responded? That was my dad, and that was when they first met."

Rose's eyes widened as she remembered that day. "Oh, my goodness. That was him? That was your dad? Amazing."

Ryan's expression grew more confused. "Gram, what is she talking about? When did my mom find a girl in the park?"

I guess Rose had never told Ryan all the stories she had told me. "Oh honey, I have a lot to tell you about your mother. I promise I'll tell you about that day, and so much more, tonight." Rose looked back at me. "Sarah, is there more you discovered?"

I shook my head. "No, that's all I came here to tell you both. I'm sorry I didn't tell you sooner. I was coping with the information myself for a while." I finished my coffee, stood up, and thanked Rose again as I began to leave.

Ryan, who had been predominately speechless until now, stopped me. "Wait, Sarah."

I turned around. "Yes?"

Ryan got out of his chair and walked up to me. Before I realized what he was doing, he had both of his arms around me. I wrapped both of my arms around him, returning the hug. To my own surprise, I felt a frog in my throat followed by my cheeks growing wet. I couldn't stop myself from letting out an uncontrollable short sob. I shoveled my tears back inside and wiped my face with my sleeve.

"Thank you so much for everything," Ryan said.

"You are very welcome. Maybe you both could come over to my Aunt Maggie's one Sunday for dinner with my dad and me."

Rose answered, "We would love that!"

Ryan agreed, "Yes, that sounds perfect."

I returned to my car and texted Matt to let him know I'd made the notification. Then, I drove to my dad's house and got Hallie. Poor Hallie was still hiding under the bed after all these hours. "Here, girl." Hallie came out and purred loudly as she wrapped her body around my legs. I gave her several scratches and let her relieve herself at her litterbox before I loaded up all of her things. I grabbed a few items of my dad's that I knew he would need over at Aunt Maggie's, figuring I would bring him back the next day to get the rest of his things.

I hit the road and noticed that the rain was finally starting to ease up. I drove down the shade way and began to let my mind wander. *We finally got her, we got Betty Ann. But who called 911 from Rose's house? Was it really Samuel? And what about the shadow figure I saw run into the basement at Patch Lane?* After everything I'd experienced the past month, I'd learned that there were some things that simply couldn't be explained. I was repeatedly drawn to this case, no matter how many times I was pushed away from it. Rose's words still lingered in my mind. *Like a moth to a flame.*

I pulled up to Aunt Maggie's house, and Hallie and I made ourselves at home. I took a long, steaming hot shower and changed into my pajamas. I sat down on the couch and covered my legs with a blanket, Hallie following suit. I heard the front door open and saw Aunt Maggie helping my dad inside. They came into the family room and my dad plopped down onto the couch next to Hallie and me while Aunt Maggie settled into her usual recliner. I got up to pour us each a glass of wine. Then, I found my way back onto the couch and snuggled with Hallie.

We turned on the late-night news and were faced with the headline "Murder Suspect Caught—Amber Forest Police Department Secretary." They showed a video clip of Chief Fox standing at a podium, addressing several reporters.

We are here to announce that an arrest has been made in the murder of Michelle Kline. The Amber Forest Police Department, working with our federal partners from the FBI, U.S. Marshals Service, and Federal Bureau of ATF, worked diligently to bring justice to the family of Michelle Kline and the Amber Forest community.

I personally want to thank all the officers that worked many long, hard hours to follow the leads and evidence in this very complex investigation that led to today's arrest. I am honored to have fully supported my officers throughout their investigation and proud to be the chief of such an incredible department.

I couldn't help but laugh at Chief Fox's speech after everything he put me through. *Fully supported my officers?* Yeah, right. I wasn't surprised that he was trying to take credit for Betty Ann's arrest, so I simply rolled my eyes and accepted that some people couldn't be changed.

I closed my eyes, took a sip of my wine, and sunk deeper into the couch. When I opened my eyes, my dad was laughing at Aunt Maggie's impersonation of Chief Fox. I watched them roar with laughter while Hallie crawled up onto my chest to snuggle even closer. I was happy to be away from work, but I also wasn't dreading the moment I would have to return. There was a sense of closure that had nestled comfortably around me, and for the first time in over a month, I let myself be present in the moment.

Acknowledgements

I would like to acknowledge everyone who made Patch Lane possible:

A special thanks to my cousin, Christine, for her unconditional support. Not only did she keep me sane throughout this process, but she helped me work through plot holes, beta read, and continuously pushed me to keep writing.

I would also like to thank my husband, my dad, and Jessica McMurray of the Allegheny County Medical Examiner's Office for sharing their expertise and corroborating procedural accuracy.

Thank you to my stepmom and friends, Laura Myers, Natalia Fenton and Eric Miller, for beta reading Patch Lane, assisting with preliminary edits, and helping me with establishing an online platform.

Thank you to all my Reddit r/NoSleep fans, including Floris Maat, for your support and motivation in transforming Patch Lane from a short story into a full-length novel.

Finally, thank you to my publisher, Between the Lines Publishing, for seeing the potential in Patch Lane.

S.F. Barkley is a former police officer who uses her law enforcement background along with her love for all things creepy to influence her writing. She has had numerous eerie experiences as a cop including discovering secret underground tunnels and responding to 911 hang up calls to an abandoned industrial building. She has published several short horror stories in various anthologies. Patch Lane is her debut novel. She was raised in Western Pennsylvania and currently resides in Maryland with her husband and their rescue pup.